Whale's
Tales

Whale's Tales

Recollections

of a

Diesel Submariner

Bruce J. Schick

Book design and production: Tabby House
Cover design: Lewis Agrell

ISBN 10: 0-9773537-0-2
ISBN 13: 978-0-9773537-0-5

Library of Congress Control Number: 2005936226

Third printing January 2007

DBF Press
2319 Goldmine Road
Louisa, VA 23093

Foreword

A mother and three small boys huddle against the wind at the Cabrillo Monument in San Diego, peering west into the Pacific mist. The year is 1967 or '68, and the object of their search appears first as a tiny wake, then the still far-off black form of a submarine running east on the surface. The sighting means only one thing to this young family— Daddy's home! The race begins to the Ballast Point submarine base and the pier, where the boys are lined up for a last-minute inspection as

the warship docks to the accompaniment of a navy band; throbbing, smoking diesels; and the organized bedlam of line handlers, families, staff officers, and well-wishers. So ends another six-month-plus WESTPAC deployment for the crew and families of *Razorback*.

5

To my brothers and me, my father's career in submarines meant Christmases and birthdays at our grandparents' and exotic gifts from mysterious ports around the globe. It meant letters and postcards complimenting our grades or athletic achievements, or occasionally admonishing us for not doing as we should. It meant new schools every few years and stretches of time with Dad at sea, punctuated by shore duty when he came home from the base long after dark and couldn't talk about his work. It was the smell of diesel oil and sweat in the laundry hamper, and dinner on crisp linens in the wardroom on the boat for special occasions. It meant the only time Mom cried more than when he left was when he returned, and we cried right along with her. Ours was a normal, loving navy family, and there were, and are, thousands like ours all around the country.

It was not until the end of the Cold War that details of the submariners' lives began to filter to those of us who shared homes with them. During one of the most turbulent times in our country's history, these men, all volunteers, quietly went about the deadly business of keeping the Russian Bear at bay. In ways most of us will never know, their missions contributed to winning the Cold War and the preservation of liberty. They were seamen first, spies second, and warriors too, who spent long periods of time in harm's way doing things they could not even share with classmates or wives. Theirs was a close fraternity of professionals who put their country and their shipmates above personal interests. The small size and shared mission of the diesel submarine force nurtured a mystic camaraderie that continues well beyond their retirement. All of the boats and many of the men are gone now. Some of those who remain are beginning to share with loved ones glimpses of what their lives as submariners were like. This book is one of those stories; it is the story of my dad, Naval Academy class of 1959, career diesel boat submariner, loving husband, father, and friend.

JOHN T. SCHICK
LOUISA, VIRGINIA

Prologue

An old naval saying:
How do you tell a sea story from a fairy tale?
A fairy tale starts, "Once upon a time."
A sea story starts, "Now this is no shit."

The Thames River flows between Groton and New London, Connecticut, just before it empties into Long Island Sound. Locals call it the *Thames*, not as the British pronounce their *Temes*. Groton, on the northern bank, is home to the U.S. Submarine Force. The submarine base is called the New London Submarine Base, despite the fact that it is on the wrong side of the river. The town of New London, on the south bank, is home to Connecticut College and the Coast Guard Academy. You figure it out.

In 1960, between the submarine base and the sound, there was a huge, great, high, arching bridge across the river for automobile traffic. There was also a low, flat bridge for trains. The railroad bridge was a drawbridge. On the bridge was a shack in which lived a little old man who raised the bridge. Vessels coming up or down the river blew their horns, the old man checked to see if a train was coming or not, and he opened the bridge or not, depending. His job was to keep trains from falling into the river. He was not paid by the submarine force; he was paid by the railroad people. He didn't give jack-shit for submarines. He also seemed, in my days on the river, to sleep a lot, or he was deaf as a stone.

A submarine, fully surfaced, could not pass under the bridge. But a submarine could submerge partially (Don't worry, the channel is deep enough.) and squeeze under the bridge. By carefully venting tanks, one

7

could take a boat down to where the decks were awash and get deep enough to clear the bridge if the old guy was taking a nap or a train was coming.

In order to make sure we were deep enough, an officer would lie on top of the sail and eyeball the bridge—a very primitive transit.

So . . . we were proceeding down the river. We blew our horn to ask the old guy to open the bridge. No response. Backing water. Current flowing fast. Rocks to starboard, rocks to port. Blow again. Still no response. Captain says, "Flood down to the water line." XO (executive officer, number two officer on board, second in command) climbs on top of the sail. We flood down. Decks awash. XO eyeballs the bridge. Says, " Okay, let's go." We sail under the bridge.

Now on top of the snorkel mast was a radio antenna called the *beer can.* Highest point on the boat. Three times as big as a real beer can. Fragile. We go under the bridge. Bump. Beer can is now at a forty-five degree angle. Oh, shit!

Skipper calls the senior radioman to the bridge. A chief petty officer—we were lucky to have one so experienced. Chief says, "What's wrong?" Captain says, "Beer can's bent. What should we do?"

Chief puts his arm around the captain and says, "Blow the boat up six inches and back up through the bridge, Skippsie. That should straighten her back in place." *Never* call the old man anything but Cap'n. "Old Man" is okay behind his back, and he'll be pleased if he overhears. But Skippsie? *Never.*

Author's note: The commanding officer of a naval ship is called captain, no matter what his actual rank. There are various ways in which one can refer to a commanding officer:

The most formal term is "commanding officer" as in "The commanding officer of USS *Cafultafish* was relieved of command immediately on discovering he could not swim." Formal written correspondence usually employs this term.

"CO" is shorthand for commanding officer. It is used in electrical message traffic (sort of like telegrams) as an official abbreviation and informally in conversation. "The CO is not on board."

"Captain," often pronounced "cap'n," is used as a salutation, as in "Good morning, Captain." The surname may be appended, as in "Good morning, Captain Jones." One also may refer to "the captain of USS

Cafultafish." This would be somewhat less formal than above, but entirely proper.

"Skipper" is a friendly sobriquet denoting affection. Most captains tolerate the term, and some actually welcome it as a sign of a subordinate's regard. Some senior officers use the term when addressing a favorite subordinate. All "captains" beam with joy when the boss calls them "skipper."

"The old man" is another term usually used by the crew to refer to their captain when talking to sailors from other ships, as in "my old man can whip your old man." Or, if everyone had to stay aboard after working hours to conduct some kind of training, one would call his wife to report "I'll be home late for supper. The old man's got a wild hair across his ass."

Merchant ships use somewhat the same terminology, but their most formal term is "master." One reads in the press of the "master of SS *Rustbucket."* Master, a term with a long pedigree, is short for "master after God." This is a reflection of the awesome power given captains in the age of sail, including the power of life or death. Many an insubordinate sailor literally was hanged from the yardarm by a master who was accuser, judge, jury, and executioner.

When I assumed command of USS *Clamagore,* I was a lieutenant commander (LCDR). I was issued a bumper sticker for the car that said "CO," my reserved parking place was labeled "COs Only," and my executive officer (XO) greeted me, "Good morning, Captain. Welcome aboard." The base newspaper reported that "LCDR B. J. Schick was the new Commanding Officer of Clamagore." The squadron commander, my boss, said, "Congratulations, Skipper." And I signed official correspondence:

B. J. SCHICK

LCDR, USN, COMMANDING

Understand all that? Don't worry, there is no quiz to come.

By the way, the chief radioman fixed the beer can after we returned to port.

If this catches your imagination, read on. What follows is a hodgepodge of memories, compiled by one of the last of the diesel sailors.

Genesis

I was born on Long Island, New York in 1937.

Among my parents' friends was a man I called Uncle El. He was no blood kin but must have been a close family friend for me to call him uncle. He was a navy warrant electrician. I don't know whether he was career navy or had been given that rather senior rank because of the war and his civilian experience. In any case, he was awesome in his dress blues. He had a bridge coat that went below his knees and had about a thousand brass buttons. At the age of three or four, I looked up at that set of blues and decided I wanted to be a naval officer when I grew up. My father was an air raid warden and wore an armband and a tin hat, but the blues won hands down.

We moved to Frederick, Maryland, when I was five. I did well in high school and never deviated from my goal of becoming a naval officer. I figured if you were going to be an officer in the navy, you might as well go to the Naval Academy. My parents had no political pull, so as soon as I turned seventeen, I joined the Naval Reserve in order to be able to take the competitive exam for the academy. In addition to the congressional political appointments, three hundred midshipmen were admitted each year from the Naval Reserves

The author with Uncle El.

11

and three hundred from the fleet.

I took the entrance exam in 1954 along with 4,000 other Naval Reservists and did well enough to win one of the three hundred appointments. Unfortunately, this academic promise did not extend through my time at Annapolis, but I was on my way.

I was graduated in 1959 and commissioned as an ensign, U.S. Navy. I stood 105 in a class of just under 700, so I was able to pick my first duty station. I chose USS *Gainard (DD 706)*, a destroyer homeported in Newport, Rhode Island.

The Heritage in Photographs

Most of my family attended graduation. A lot of photographs were taken. Grandparents, parents, aunts and uncles. My maternal grandparents, the Quinns, look proud in the photos. Neither of them got beyond the fifth grade. My parents look somewhat bewildered. Neither of them had graduated from high school, and they may have been questioning the forces they had unleashed. My fiancée, Pat, pinning on my new shoulder boards, just looks in love. I was not only the first of my family to graduate from college, I was graduating from the United States Naval Academy, a very prestigious school.

Pat gave me a sword. Inscribed on it was a biblical quotation, "Whither thou goest, I will go." Her inscription was to be prophetic. Kurt, number three son, and the only one of our sons to serve in the navy, now has the sword. But it lives in my heart.

Gainard (DD 706)

After graduation and a wonderful wedding, my new bride and I drove to Newport to set up housekeeping. I had thirty days leave and then was to proceed to Guantanamo Bay, Cuba, to join my first ship. I had picked *Gainard* because she was just out of overhaul and would be operating at sea. No sitting alongside the pier for me! After our month of newlywed bliss, I reported to the Naval Air Station at Quonset Point for a ride to Gitmo (Guantanamo Bay) and *Gainard.* I never even thought of leaving a brand-new bride all by herself in a strange town. Never occurred to me. I knew she could handle herself. Of such confidence come strong marriages—or quick divorces.

USS *Gainard (DD706). Official U.S. Navy photo, courtesy of Richard Leonhardt.*

Courier Duty

While en route from Newport to Gitmo, I had a layover at the Naval Air Station in Norfolk. The public address system suddenly summoned Ensign Schick to the duty officer's desk. On reporting, I was told I had been selected as a courier to accompany classified information to Gitmo. I was issued a .38 caliber revolver, six rounds of ammunition, and three or four large, sealed, canvas mailbags. The bags, I was told, were full of highly classified secret stuff. I was to guard them with my life. The mailbags would occupy seats adjoining my own. No problem!

The aircraft loaded in due time. Passengers were mostly dependent wives and children—lots of children. Active, noisy, curious children. And there I sat with my mailbags and a loaded pistol in a shoulder holster. All the little boys were fascinated by the gun, but I held them off. For all I knew, they could have been midget Communist spies. Finally we were airborne. Then we circled. Then we dumped fuel. Then we landed back at Norfolk. Mechanical trouble. It would take a few hours to repair. Everyone but me and my mailbags left the aircraft. It got hotter and hotter out there on the tarmac. The door to the head (a restroom in the navy) was locked. I had to pee. I leaned out the door and asked a passerby to ask the duty officer to send someone by.

Pretty soon a sailor showed up and said the duty officer had sent him. I gave him the gun, told him to watch the bags, and went into the terminal to relieve myself. Bought a Coke and some Nabs (Nabisco cheese and peanut butter crackers to you Yankees) and returned to the aircraft. There was the sailor, looking very sheepish and the same Duty Officer, looking very upset. He informed me I had abandoned my post and left a firearm adrift. I respectfully informed him I had turned both the post and the firearm over to the selfsame sailor he had provided. He informed me I was going to be court-martialed. I was terrified, to say the least.

This duty officer, a full lieutenant who I knew spoke only to God, must have seen, or smelled, my fear. After what seemed an eternity, he said that seeing I was so green he would take pity and drop all charges. He admonished me to pay closer attention and left.

Finally we landed in Gitmo, with all the women and children hot, sweaty, and tired. The door opened and in came an officer and two sailors with submachine guns. Maybe those little boys were Communist spies after all. Anyway, we got the bags off, I turned over the damn pistol, and went to find *Gainard*. What a trip!

First Division Officer

I was one of four brand-new ensigns in *Gainard* (officers always serve *in* ships, not *on* ships), and the only Academy graduate. It was assumed I knew more than my ROTC or OCS comrades, and I was immediately given the First Division. Twenty-two years old and in charge of twenty-odd men. The First Division was responsible for the five-inch guns and everything topside forward of amidships. This included the anchor, windlass, decks, bulkheads, superstructure, lifelines, paintwork, brass, and so forth. The division leading petty officer was a chief gunner's mate named Campigato. He was a World War II veteran old enough to be my father.

Every morning at quarters, Chief Campigato would salute smartly. I would return the salute. Then I would ask him what we were supposed to do that day. He would then take charge and give directions to our sailors. I had no idea what had to be done in the daily routine of a deck division on an operating man of war. Hadn't been taught that at Annapolis.

Things went pretty well, and after a month or so, I was given additional duty as first lieutenant. The first lieutenant was responsible for all of topside. Both the first (me) and second division officers reported to the first lieutenant for duty on matters topside, and to the gunnery officer for matters pertaining to the guns.

First Class Boatswain Mate Stokes was the leading petty officer for the first lieutenant. Like Chief Campigato, he had been around a long time. He should have been a chief, but the boatswain rate had been frozen for years, and there just were no promotions. Stokes was one of the most squared-away sailors I ever served with. Like Chief Campigato, he saluted respectfully and then helped (guided?) me through the day.

I didn't know it until years later, but Campigato and Stokes were waiting to see if I was worth saving. At some moment in time, the votes were in and I passed muster. Then they started to train me to be an officer.

Chief Campigato's wife invited Pat and me by for dinner. It was unheard of for an officer to be invited to a chief's home. We were introduced to other chiefs and their wives. We met their children. We drank their beer. We learned how to be productive members of the navy family. I don't know what ever happened to Chief Campigato after he retired, but I like to think he somehow got into teaching. He had little formal education, but he had all the right moves.

We couldn't get Stokes a chief's hat, so we did the next best thing. We got him a commission. He became, somewhat against his will, Ensign Stokes. More on Stokes later.

In those days, good petty officers knew a large part of their job was to train young officers. Both Campigato and Stokes were masters of the art.

The Laundry

We had a laundry on board. Hot, dirty work. I think two sailors ran it. One was from Frederick, Maryland, my hometown. Although we had not known each other back home, I guess he had some bragging rights with other crewmembers. Anyway, he was very helpful and friendly to me.

Officers and chiefs wore wash khakis at sea. Stiffly starched, compliments of the laundry. At Annapolis, we wore fresh khakis every day. On hot, muggy days, we might change during the day. Spit and polish. On *Gainard,* I limited my changes to once a day.

After six months or so, my laundry friend got up the courage to ask, "Mr. Schick, could you manage to wear a set of khakis for maybe two days? It gets awfully hot in there." I was very embarrassed and immediately complied with his request.

Just a few years later I was wearing a set of khakis for a month at a time in the submarine force and turning my underwear inside out once a week to get two weeks out of it.

How times change!

Dunkin' Dickey

The gunnery officer (Gun Boss) was a lieutenant jg (junior grade) named Dick Duncan. He took some leave and went off to be married. It was late summer. Very hot. We sent him a telegram:

"When the frost is on the punkin',
That's the time for dickey dunkin'.
When the weather's hot and sticky,
That's no time for dunkin' dickey."

Another Wedding

Another of our messmates decided to tie the knot. Big fancy wedding in Boston. Most of the wardroom were involved as ushers. Dress whites and swords. We drove up the night before for the rehearsal dinner. Great party. Lots of booze. Friends of the bride put us up in private homes. Woke up the next morning, hungover, but raring to go.

Took a quick shower and started to dress. No white socks! My host had none, but he did have a bottle of white shoe polish. Problem solved—paint your ankles. Looked just like socks.

No white gloves. No problem . . . get all the other guys to go barehanded.

No hat. Wouldn't need it in church, anyway. Get everybody to go bareheaded for the arch of swords after the ceremony. The bride wouldn't know the difference.

No sword belt. The sword would be in the scabbard during the ceremony. Just carry it in the left hand and fake it.

Nice wedding. Never had to pack a bag to travel again; the better half took care of everything from that day on.

The Sword and the Awning

Commander Destroyer Force Atlantic (abbreviated as COMDESLANT) was coming to *Gainard* for a formal inspection. We took weeks to get ready. Everything was cleaned, shined, and repainted. There were to be sideboys and an honor guard on the quarterdeck. The honor guard would consist of an officer with sword, a petty officer with sidearm, and eight sailors with rifles.

A naval marching formation has been described (mostly by Marines) as "a bunch of sailors going in the same general direction at about the same time." Close order drill and the manual of arms were certainly not our forte. As a recent Academy graduate, I was proficient in handling a sword, and, God knows, knew how to march. So I was designated as the officer-in-charge and told to teach our bunch of rowdies how to look smart. They drew weapons from the armory, and we drilled on the pier until we were at least presentable.

Meanwhile, we had a new canvas awning made for the quarterdeck. The awning was scrubbed numerous times with salt water and left in the sun to bleach. It sparkled.

We had many drills on the quarterdeck with our honor guard until the XO was satisfied.

Finally the day arrives. The admiral is coming at noon. Bright and early, we wet the new awning once again with saltwater and string it tightly over the quarterdeck. The sun will shrink it as it dries, and it will be as tight as a drumhead. The honor guard dons our best uniforms. Our whites sparkle. Our brass glitters. Our shoes look like patent leather. Just time enough left for a final dress rehearsal.

We fall in on the quarterdeck. The XO gives the first order: "Present arms."

Just as I had been taught at Annapolis, I rotate the sword ninety degrees clockwise and bring the hilt up smartly to my chin, the blade at a perfect forty-five degree angle . . . right through the awning. Sounds like a fat man bending over in too-tight trousers. The canvas is under so much tension, the rip immediately spreads three feet.

Too late. The admiral's car is on the pier. We pipe him aboard, render honors, and he never looks up at the torn awning. I spent a week in hack (confined to quarters).

Rendering Honors

When two naval vessels pass in the channel, the junior renders honors to the senior. This time-honored courtesy dates back to the age of sail. It is similar to a junior person saluting a senior, except the entire ship renders honors.

The ranking of the ships is determined by the relative seniority of their captains. As the approaching ship is identified, one looks up the skipper in a registry and determines if he is senior to ours. As the bows cross, the junior ship's bo'sun sounds "attention to port/starboard." All hands topside come to attention and face the appropriate side. As the bow crosses the bridge, the bo'sun orders, "Hand Salute." After the senior vessel has returned the salute, the bo'sun orders, "To," and "Carry on." Simple.

The relative seniority of the skippers is overridden when a flag officer (admiral) is embarked in one of the ships. The admiral's flag is flown from a yardarm, and his becomes the senior ship. His flag reflects the number of stars to which he is entitled. Officers of the line, that is, those eligible to command at sea, fly a blue flag with white stars. Staff officers (doctors, lawyers, supply corps, etc.) fly a white flag with blue stars. Marines fly a red flag.

To be very truthful, line officers kinda looked down on the others. Wherein lies the tale.

I had the deck coming into port. A smaller, junior ship was putting out to sea. It was flying a white, two star flag. I did not render honors. We passed, with the other ship all lined up waiting for our salute. Nothing. Nada. A furious radio message soon arrived, and our furious XO arrived on the bridge.

"Mr. Schick, did you see the admiral's flag on that ship we just passed?" he asked.

"Yes, sir." I said.

"Why then, did you not render honors?"

"It was only a staff officer, not a line officer, sir."

Another week in hack.

Author's note: When an officer is put "in hack," he is restricted to the ship if in port and usually to his cabin if at sea. He normally is allowed out only to stand watches and take his meals. In the old days, he would surrender his sword as a symbol of his disgrace.

I never had to surrender my sword while in *Gainard*.

Bull Halsey

Most new ensigns went directly from college or OCS (Officer Candidate School) to sea. The theory was a young man ought to get some saltwater under his keel right off the bat. We acquired the exception to the rule.

A new lieutenant junior grade arrived on board, fresh from a tour in the Pentagon. He had been there two years as a security officer. This was to be his first sea tour. He was assigned as second division officer. I, an ensign, was still first lieutenant. Hence, although he was senior to me, I was his boss. Trouble brewing.

By now, I was qualified as a fleet OD (officer of the deck). This meant I stood top watch on the bridge without supervision when we were underway. The JOD (junior officer of the deck) stood instruction watches under the supervision of the OD. Our new jg, whom we had nicknamed Bull after the famed Admiral Bull Halsey, had to stand instruction watches under an ensign. More trouble.

We usually let the JOD drive the ship. In navy parlance, he had the conn. He gave orders to the helmsman to come right or left, and to the engine room to speed up or slow down. When an oncoming JOD had relieved his off-going counterpart, he saluted the OD and reported that he had relieved so-and-so and assumed the conn. Not Bull! He refused to salute an ensign.

In short order, the entire crew came to hate poor Bull. As the saying goes, most sailors aboard *Gainard* had rung more saltwater out of their jock straps than he had sailed over, but he simply knew *everything*. Learned it in the Pentagon.

The Wheel

Gainard's rudder was normally controlled by a large wooden steering wheel with brass spokes. The wheel was located on the bridge and manned by the helmsman. It controlled powerful electric motors that actually moved the rudder.

After Steering was located all the way in the stern. It was a small, cramped compartment, where, if main steering failed, the rudder could be controlled by applying sailor-power. In an emergency, we manned the sound-powered phones, disengaged the normal steering mechanism, and gave rudder orders over the phones to the guys back aft. We routinely practiced this procedure. And it was expected that the OD would conduct routine training exercises when time and circumstances permitted. Starting to get the drift?

The middle of the night. The middle of the ocean. Steaming independently. No other ships in sight. Bull is the oncoming JOD. Setup time!

Quickly, now. Shift control to After Steering. Take out the pin that fastened the wheel to its shaft. No giggles!

Bull arrives on the bridge. Gets all the info from his predecessor. Assumes the conn. Reports to the OD. Salutes! My, he is learning.

Helmsman comes up to Bull carrying the now disconnected steering wheel and asks what he should do. Steering wheel fell off. Panic! Entire watch section is breaking up with laughter. Poor Bull!

Lesson Number Two: The Boat

Gainard had a motor whaleboat. It hung from davits which were usually swung inboard. If the boat was to be lowered into the water, the davits were swung outboard so the boat would clear the ship's side when it was lowered away into the water. The boat was secured to the ship by a line from its bow to the main deck. This line is called a sea painter. Normally the boat would be lowered while making three knots or less, so that it was not sucked up against the hull.

Entering San Juan, Puerto Rico. No room at the naval base. Have to moor across the harbor at a coal pier. Skipper wants to use the whaleboat to go across the harbor to the base, rather than have to drive around and cross the bridge. Quicker to the officers' club. Good thinking.

The second division officer (poor Bull) is in charge of the boat. Orders the davits swung out. No problem. Orders the boat made ready to launch. Sea painter is attached, etc. No problem. Orders the boat lowered. Wait! We're doing fifteen knots. Bo'sun, grinning all the while, lowers the boat. Splinters! Towing a few pieces of broken wood, all that's left of the whaleboat.

XO arrives on scene. Asks the bo'sun, "Why in God's name did you lower the boat when we were doing fifteen knots?"

Bo'sun replies, "Lieutenant Bull told me to." How sweet it was. And that's all I have to say about poor Bull Halsey. Maybe he went on to become a successful civilian lawyer.

A Submarine Comes to Newport

When *Gainard* was entering port, the OD would retain the conn (drive the ship) until we passed the sea buoy at the harbor mouth. Then the captain would come to the bridge and take over. On rare occasions, he would let the XO drive for training purposes. This was pretty much standard procedure in the Destroyer Fleet.

One day we were moored at the pier and were told to standby to take a submarine alongside. As she approached, I was amazed to see that her skipper was standing on top of the sail and a junior officer, a lieutenant jg, was driving. Unheard of! The skipper was watching him, to be sure, but that young officer actually was doing the driving.

That evening, the submarine wardroom came aboard *Gainard* to watch the evening movie. I asked about this amazing occurrence and was told junior officers routinely brought submarines alongside. "How else were they to learn?" I was hooked. You had to be a lieutenant commander to be given that much responsibility and trust in a destroyer.

At that time, you had to be a qualified fleet OD (I was) and have been in destroyers for at least a year before you could apply for submarine school. Because of the rapid expansion of the nuclear submarine force, submarine school was going from two to four classes a year. As a result, the one-year requirement was waived in the spring of 1960. I applied, was accepted, and in March 1960, was on my way to sub school.

One Last Tale before We Leave the Surface Navy

I loved the navigation courses at the Academy and did well. First class (senior) year my instructor was a lieutenant who was returning to sea duty at the completion of the academic year. He was going to a destroyer homeported in Newport, and he told me to look him up when I got there.

Arriving in Newport after our honeymoon, we found our few household furnishings were still somewhere on a moving truck. We rented a motel room and settled down to wait.

I called up my former instructor, and we were invited over for dinner. When he and his wife found we were living in a motel, nothing would do but that we move in with them. We did, and their small children slept on the living room floor while we occupied the nursery.

As we were leaving, Pat said to our hostess, "I wish there were some way we could pay you back for your hospitality." Our gracious hostess replied, "In the navy, we don't pay back. We give back. Your opportunities will come."

How many times in the future did we give and receive the same kindnesses. The navy family was a close and caring one.

Submarine School

Officers' Submarine School was an arduous, six-month course taught at the Submarine Base in New London, Connecticut. We students were all twenty-three or twenty-four years old, and the large majority were bachelors.

The bachelors lived in the BOQ (bachelor officers' quarters) two blocks from the sub school. There were a limited number of married officers' quarters (MOQ). Those couples who were pregnant got first dibs on the MOQ, and then the unpregnant couples drew straws until the quarters were filled up. Anyone still left had to fend for themselves out in town, an expensive proposition. The married quarters, six blocks from the school, were an easy walk and much preferable to living on the economy (off-base}.

Quarters consisted of attached brick houses. There were two small bedrooms upstairs and a living-dining room and kitchen down. Small, but adequate.

The Train

Life in the MOQ was good. We weren't rich, but we weren't too poor either. I was making $222.22 a month plus an allowance for food. We studied hard all day and had great amounts of homework, but we were all volunteers marching towards the same goal . . . the Submarine Force. We knew everything we were studying was important; no elective courses here. We were all young and in love. Most of the wives were in various stages of pregnancy, and some already had a child or two. The ones with children were former enlisted men who had been commissioned. The few who were not pregnant were readily accepted. And herein lies the tale of the train.

The railroad tracks were just across the road from the quarters. Trains ran right through the base on a regular schedule. One came through every morning at 5:30. You know how punctual trains used to be. When the train (it was a freight) came through, it blew its whistle and rumbled so that the entire quarters shook. Naturally, it woke everyone up. But it was too early to get up and start the day. And it was too late to go back to sleep. So . . . by the end of the six-month curriculum, *every* wife was pregnant. How else to occupy our time?

Beds and Baseboards

The quarters were furnished; that is, they had the basic furniture and appliances necessary to set up housekeeping.

As I said earlier, the rooms were quite small. In one of our upstairs bedrooms the door could not be closed because the bed was in the way. The bed needed to be moved only an inch or so, but the baseboard prevented doing so.

Now, I had an engineering degree from the United States Naval Academy, an accredited institution of some standing. Furthermore, I believed then, and still do, in three basic philosophies:

1. If the book does not say you may not do something, then you may.

2. If you take a problem to the big man, you have a big problem.

3. It is usually better to ask forgiveness than permission.

So, without further ado, out came the saw. Don't ask permission, just modify the baseboard. Hide the sawdust and little piece of lumber in the garbage. Then you can move the bed. Close the door whenever you want. Destruction of government property? Nah. Innovative problem solving.

Wilbur

With me at school all day and studying four or five hours every night, my roommate got to feeling somewhat neglected. Pregnant women do odd things. We noticed some of our neighbors had pets. Maybe a dog would be nice. Keep Pat company. But we had only a little bit of discretionary income, so it was off to the pound.

The New London Animal Shelter was located in a very dirty barnyard on what I know now to be a very slovenly farm. There were a bunch of dogs on chains, all deep in cow shit. The town paid the farmer so much a head to board the poor beasts until they were claimed or put down. It wasn't pretty, but we found a pup that looked OK and took her home. She was a walking fleabag. I mean *covered*. So we got some dip, cleaned her up, and she turned out to be the most grateful, loving, well-behaved dog we ever had. She never forgot that farm.

Pat wasn't showing much yet. She was at the three-safety-pin-let-out-the-waistband stage. We had a neighbor who was pretty well along. I mean *big*. Looked like she'd swallowed a watermelon. Her husband kept calling their unborn child Wilbur. We didn't know whether ours would be a boy or girl; this was well before the days of sonograms. But Pat was scared to death I'd think Wilbur was funny and do something silly while she was still on the delivery table. So she named the dog Wilbur. Name's already taken, right? Can't have two Wilburs in the same family. Dog never seemed to mind, even though she was a female.

Wilbur became the toast of the neighborhood. She loved everyone, and everyone loved her.

The Eggs

Three doors up was a family with two small children. He had been enlisted before he got his commission. He was a few years older than we and much more mature. Time in the fleet as a rag-hat does that to you. He was also extremely conscientious and studied at every available minute.

Every morning, Wilbur would be let out the kitchen door to do her thing. She would wander along the back of the quarters checking out the garbage cans and greeting our neighbors. Three doors up, a harried young wife would be feeding breakfast to two children and a husband with his nose in a book. It was some time before we discovered that Wilbur would stand on their back steps while the kids smushed their scrambled eggs through the screen door for her to lick. The wife never complained. Guess it kept the kids quiet while the husband got in that last few minutes of cramming.

Permission to Come Up

When a diesel boat was running on the surface, three people were required on the bridge: the officer of the deck and two lookouts. The OD could allow visitors at his discretion. Sailors loved to go topside to get a breath of fresh air. Because the OD was responsible for making sure no one was left on the bridge when the boat submerged, prospective visitors would call up through the conning tower hatch "Permission to come up?" By maintaining positive control of who came up, the OD could keep an accurate count to make sure everybody got below when the boat submerged. We were learning all this stuff in class.

Most of us in the MOQ used the spare bedroom as a study room. One of our classmates, if he was upstairs studying, required his wife to request "permission to come up" even to go to the bathroom. Good practice for him; good training for her.

Bridge

Most of us had played bridge in college. We continued at Sub School. It was a cheap form of entertainment. It was not unusual to have two or three tables of a Saturday night. Each couple brought a six-pack of beer, and the hosts provided potato chips and pretzels.

The men would cheat. If you drew a zip hand, you would look at your partner, if he was a man, throw down your cards, and say, "I've got fourteen cards." He would quickly reply "I've got twelve. Misdeal," and throw his down.

Drove the wives crazy.

Ice Cream and Sex

Our refrigerators had the old-fashioned little ice cube boxes which held four or five ice trays and nothing more. One of our classmates lucked out and had a brand-new refrigerator with a full-size freezer chest on top. We all kept our ice cream in his freezer.

They were one of the few couples who were not pregnant, but were trying hard. Every Sunday afternoon their window shades would go down, and their front door would be locked. But their kitchen door lock didn't work. Beginning to see what's coming?

As soon as the shades went down, the word would spread, and the ice cream parade would start. Open the back door, go through the kitchen into the living room, and holler up the stairs, "Don't come down. I'm only getting some ice cream." Three or four of us in a row. Lined up on the back porch giggling, waiting our turn. Funny thing is, they never told us to take our ice cream and shove it. We were beginning to be a tight group. And she got pregnant.

Underway

Finally, it was time for the first exercise. We split into groups of six or eight students and an instructor, and boarded submarines for a week at sea. We were thrilled and scared to death. On the diving simulators at Sub School, we had crashed into the sea floor, sunk innumerable times, opened the wrong valves, and generally screwed up while learning to dive one of these beasts. But nobody had drowned. This was the real thing.

A submarine on the surface rides on a cushion of air. Take an empty water cup, invert it, and push it down into a bowl of water. See how the water comes up into the cup only part way, and air is trapped in the top? Now punch a hole in the bottom of the cup and try the same thing. The water fills the cup as the air escapes through the hole. That's how a submarine works.

On the surface, special tanks called ballast tanks are full of air, except for a water seal on the bottom. They are open to the sea on the bottom, just like your cup. At the top are vent valves which normally are closed. When they are opened, the air escapes out the top, the water comes in the bottom, the air cushion goes out through the vents as the tanks fill, and the submarine submerges.

In World War II, we learned we had to submerge as quickly as possible to avoid attack. In order to minimize the time until fully under water, diesel boats would start to submerge while the men were still on the bridge. Nuclear boats (nucs) don't do it this way because they don't spend much time on the surface. The diesel boat diving sequence is thus:

The skipper calls the OD and says, "Submerge the ship."

The OD orders: "Clear the bridge," while sounding two blasts on the Klaxon.

The lookouts scramble below.

On the second blast of the Klaxon, the vents are opened, and the boat starts to sink.

The OD makes sure everybody has preceded him, slides down the ladder, and shuts the hatch. He then proceeds down another deck and becomes the diving officer. By the time he takes control of the dive, the boat is already at thirty feet or so and sinking fast.

What a thrill. I'll never forget that first dive on a real submarine!

The Nucs

Halfway through the course, the dozen or so top students were summoned by Admiral Rickover to be interviewed. Rickover was in charge of the Navy Nuclear Power Program. He selected a half dozen and told each he could go to nuclear power training if he graduated first in the class. This was my first exposure to the *Rickover method*. Obviously, only one of these guys would finish first.

What had been a competitive but collegial class now contained a subset of prospective nucs who had a different agenda. The class joke was that if you dropped your pencil on the floor during an exam, one of the pre-nucs would kick it out of your reach.

Only one of these fired-up achievers finished first, of course. But Rickover took them all, as he had planned all along. My point is, his approach to life as an officer violated all that we had been taught at Annapolis. We had learned to look out for our shipmates first, then ourselves. That was not the Rickover way.

House Hunting

We were due to graduate in September, and the baby was due in October. In view of the difficulty in traveling that late in a pregnancy, the navy told me I would be assigned to a New London boat. So the serious nest-building began.

Pat had a small inheritance from a great-uncle, so she decided we would buy a house rather than rent. We made two lists: needs and wants. The former included such things as two bedrooms, running water, heat, a kitchen, etc. The latter included a corner lot, established shrubbery, a fireplace, and some other stuff I can't recall. We asked around and approached a well-recommended Realtor. His initial observation was that ensigns don't buy houses. When he saw the needs and wants lists, he actually laughed. Pat persisted, however, and he rather reluctantly showed us a few houses. They were dogs! We were ready to give up when he said he had one more offering, but we probably wouldn't like it.

It was on older Cape Cod on a corner lot. It had established (nay, overgrown) shrubbery, and a fireplace. It belonged to another naval officer who wanted someone to buy it and assume his mortgage. Sold.

We still had a month of school left, and Pat was seven months gone. The former occupant had painted lurid murals on the walls, which were themselves rather bright. The place looked like a carnival side-show. I was busy in school, but pregnant Pat sanded down the murals and repainted the whole house. Made curtains. Trimmed shrubbery. The works. By the time we moved in, the neighbors already loved her. Paid $15,000 for the house and assumed a four and a half percent mortgage. It was an in-service loan, so the navy paid a half percent.

Recently paid $21,000 for a pickup truck. How times change.

On to the Fleet

As graduation neared, I chose USS *Irex (SS482)*. She was an old fleet boat, not the most modern. But she was in the Philadelphia Naval Shipyard undergoing overhaul and was due out by Christmas. Thus almost my entire tour, nominally two years, would be spent at sea. I did not join the navy to sit alongside a pier!

USS *Irex SS482 entering Livorno, Italy. Photo courtesy of Vincent Flaherty.*

Irex was a fleet snorkel submarine. She had been built late in World War II. She was one of the earliest postwar conversions and lacked most of the more modern improvements found on other diesel boats in service at the time

At the end of WWII, the German U-boats were much more sophisticated than our submarines. We copied and improved on their designs, and upgraded our boats in various ways. In general the upgraded boats were called GUPPIES (Greater Underwater Propulsion). In order to improve their underwater performance, some reduction in surface capability was accepted. The original cruiser-type bow was replaced by a rounded one. The streamlined bow increased underwater speed and reduced noise, but limited surface speed. The batteries used for submerged propulsion were doubled, in some cases at the expense of removing one of the four diesel engines. Again, these changes increased submerged speed at the expense of surface speed. A fairwater, called a sail, was added around the old superstructure to streamline it and reduce underwater flow noise.

Irex was not a GUPPY, but was a very early experimental conversion. We kept our big fleet bow and, as a result, could do twenty-seven knots on the surface. We kept all four of our Fairbanks Morse diesel engines. And we had the very first snorkel in the U.S. Navy, copied from a German U-boat. It was primitive by the 1960 standards, but it worked.

Ensigns and Railroad Tracks

In the late 1950s and early 1960s, ensigns were promoted to lieutenants junior grade after serving eighteen months. Before the newly relaxed submarine school requirements, you will recall, one had to do a year on a surface ship before going to sub school, and the school was six months. Do the arithmetic, and you will see that an ensign had not been seen on a submarine since WWII—until now. I reported aboard *Irex* for duty wearing my shiny gold bars (called brown bars), and there at the wardroom table sat four full lieutenants wearing shiny silver double bars (called railroad tracks). Ominous. Felt like plebe year at the Academy all over again. Moreover, on their left breasts were gold dolphins, signifying they were qualified in submarines. I knew deep down in my little ensign's heart that I was in for a tough time ahead.

I would like to say they welcomed me with open arms. They didn't. They were all Naval Academy graduates . . . every officer on board was . . . and they saw a chance to play "plebes" all over again. A plebe is a freshman at the Naval Academy. Plebe year was a time of indoctrination and intimidation, not necessarily in that order. Upperclassmen, with the full blessing of the administration, tried hard to make you pack your bags and go home. The saying is they took away all your rights and gave them back one at a time, calling them privileges. Plebe year is designed to weed out those midshipmen who are not up to the rigors of navy life. It is a sometimes cruel, but effective system. My class lost a quarter of its members the first year, even after the tough entrance requirements.

Anyway, Plebe Year Number Two was about to begin.

Supply and Commissary Officer

Surface ships have supply corps officers assigned as part of their regular compliment. They are trained in all matters logistic. With only ten officers, submarines could not afford the luxury of a supply corps officer, so the junior officer on board became supply and commissary officer until someone junior to him reported aboard.

So here I was—a line officer, eligible for command at sea—a graduate of the U.S. Naval Academy and Submarine School—a trained killer—but, alas, *an ensign*. Supply and commissary officer. Counting paper clips. Making up menus. Inspecting the cooks' fingernails. Ordering toilet paper.

The guy I relieved was leaving *Irex* having failed to qualify in submarines after a couple of years. He was being sent back to the surface fleet in some disgrace. The ship was in overhaul in the Philadelphia Naval Shipyard, and every spare part had been moved to a warehouse for inventory. I signed for custody of I knew not what, and my predecessor departed.

Meanwhile, over at the warehouse all the bits and pieces of spare parts were lying around in hundreds of gunny sacks. My storekeeper, the only person on board who had any formal supply training, had been augmented by about ten regular sailors. They were a surly lot. They had been picked from the various ship's factions with an interest in spare parts: torpedomen, enginemen, electricians, sonarmen, electronics technicians, and so forth. They were in the warehouse against their will. After all, they were trained killers, too, and they had been relegated to cataloging spare parts. We had long computer lists of what we were supposed to have. We counted what we had. We compared the two. And then we ordered the shortfall. Sounds easy, but salt air, moisture, and mold had taken their toll, and many of the parts no longer had a recognizable navy stock number attached. It was a constant: "What in the hell is this?" I suspect many of the unrecognizable parts were quietly thrown into the harbor. Moreover, the computer lists were generated by punch-card technology and left much to be desired.

My commissary duties were undemanding. I had a great leading cook who made up the menus and an XO who diddled with them, so I just took the suggested bill of fair for the next week from the cook, initialed it, and gave it to the XO. He changed it; argued directly with the cook; they reached a compromise; and that was that. The skipper had a rule that anybody who bitched about the food got to be commissary officer for the next month. That helped a lot.

We finally ordered all the spare parts, stowed everything back on board, and headed back to New London, arriving just a few days before Christmas. But the books didn't balance. Out of tens of thousands of dollars, I was off a few hundred. This was due mostly to changing prices within the navy supply system. You would order at one price and when the part came in the price had changed from the catalog price. If the revised price was posted properly there was no problem. But if the storekeeper failed to notice the change, the books would not balance. With hundreds of parts arriving every week it was easy to miss a few changes.

I worked. I slaved. I was scared to death of the XO. He told me as he left the boat on December 23 that I could go home for Christmas after the books were balanced. Our first Christmas with our new son, John. The XO was some kind of nice guy!

In the dark of the night, I made out six or seven bogus supply chits with a total value to balance the books. I figured it would be too obvious to have one chit match the discrepancy, but several with random dollar amounts would make the system as crazy as it had made me. It worked. The XO came in on Christmas Eve, looked at my newly balanced books, and complimented me on my diligence. I went home. I wonder if the navy supply system ever figured it out?

Permission To Go Ashore

Working hours in port were 7:30 to 4:00. At the end of the day one would report to the XO and get his permission to go home. With the more senior officers this was no more than a formality, but with someone as junior as I, the XO would give me a little quiz to make sure I had done a full day's work. In the shipyard we all left as a group and went up to the BOQ for a beer, so the subject of requesting permission had not arisen.

Now, back in New London, I approached the XO and requested permission to go ashore. After the little quiz, he said, "Permission denied," and went home himself. After he had been gone for a while, the duty officer told me to go home. Next day, "Request permission to go ashore," quiz, and "Permission denied." A little while later the duty officer, different guy from yesterday, tells me to go home. This went on for several days. I was spending an extra hour or so on board every day. Finally a duty officer told me, "Tomorrow, don't request permission the go ashore. Instead, request permission to leave the ship."

Next day. "Permission to leave the ship?"

"Granted. You finally figured out I don't care where you go after you leave the ship."

Forty years later and it still rankles. I recently saw him at the skipper's funeral, and he's still an asshole.

Checking the Intake Pipes

Back to the shipyard.

Submarines underwent extensive six-month shipyard overhauls every three or four years. Between overhauls, repairs were accomplished at the submarine base during periodic scheduled upkeep periods of one or two weeks. Work was done by the crew and shops at the sub base. The overhauls took care of major stuff beyond the capacity of sub base or crew. They always included time in dry dock to scrape and repaint the hull and the interiors of tanks, renew the zincs, repack the shaft seals, etc.

There were four, eighteen-inch diameter pipes going aft toward the engine rooms from the main air intake valve/snorkel mast. They were in flanged, bolted sections. The two to the forward engine room were about forty feet long; to the after engine room about sixty-five feet. We had had them removed, sandblasted, and repainted. After they were reinstalled, the engineer wanted them inspected to make sure there were no leaks. The most efficient way to do this was to crawl their length, *inside* them, and look for daylight.

In those days, I weighed 140 pounds. And . . . I was an ensign. So they gave me a flashlight, tied a piece of line around my waist, and in I went. Turned the flashlight off and proceeded aft. The engineer walked alongside, outside the damned pipe, and every once in a while, he'd bang on the pipe and inquire, "You OK in there?"

Talk about claustrophobia! To make matters worse, traces of diamond dust which had been used for sandblasting remained in the pipes. I was stirring it up and breathing it in as I scuffed along on my back (there was not enough room to get up on hands and knees). My lungs felt like they were on fire.

No leaks. Job done. What would OSHA say today?

Sea Trials

Christmas was coming, and the skipper was moving heaven and hell to get us home in time for the holidays. Finally all that was left was to go out for sea trials to make sure everything was working properly.

Off we went. Cold as a whore's heart. No matter for me. I was finally going to sea in my own submarine. Everything worked great, and we headed back to Philadelphia to load the last of the stuff. Back home for the holidays. Spirits were soaring.

When preparing to enter port, ships set the special sea and anchor detail. On a submarine, an officer, usually the torpedo officer, a chief petty officer, and a couple of sailors go out on deck. They activate the forward capstan so that number one mooring line can be handled, take the lines out of the line lockers and arrange them on deck, and make the anchor ready for letting go. The anchor is made ready so in case the ship should lose steering in a narrow channel, it could be dropped to prevent running aground.

The shipyard provides its own mooring lines, so all we had to do was make ready the anchor and capstan. We would need only an officer and the chief. Water was breaking over the bow and freezing. We were coated with two inches of ice. It was really cold. But no problem for the torpedo officer . . . we had an *ensign* on board. Moreover, the ensign had been first lieutenant, in charge of the anchor and capstan on a destroyer, so he was eminently qualified. After all, a destroyer's anchor and capstan are much bigger than a submarine's.

The chief and I bundled up, got into safety belts, found a couple of hatchets, and crawled out on deck. There is a track built into the deck, and we wore safety belts with a heavy piece of line and a steel device on the end that attached to and slid along the track. On our hands and knees, we chopped ice, fastened to the track, and crawled to the bow, chopping as we went.

When we got back to the shipyard, the hospital corpsman issued us some medicinal brandy. Never worked so hard for a drink in my life. And we got home for Christmas.

Promotion

Officers are chosen for promotion by selection boards. The boards review their records and compile a list which is sent to the U.S. Senate for its consent and then to the president for approval. Thus, officers are promoted "by and with the consent of the Senate" and serve "at the pleasure of the president." As one gets further up the line, smaller numbers are needed to fill the requirements of the navy . . . we need thousands of ensigns but only a couple hundred admirals so some officers are not promoted. In navy parlance, they are "passed over" and their careers are done. Each year, the Secretary of the Navy determines the requirements and instructs the boards.

The exception to this procedure is promotion to lieutenant junior grade. Since there are so many and their evaluation time has been so short, the Bureau of Personnel sends out a blanket order to promote all ensigns on a specified date.

I noticed a bunch of my classmates wandering around the sub base sporting their new half-stripes and silver bars. They were lieutenants junior grade. I was unaware of the selection procedure described above. I thought there would be a directive to *Irex* from on high saying "Promote Schick" or something like that. Went around for weeks worrying myself sick.

One day the skipper of another submarine asked me where my new stripe was. I said we had not yet received notification. He told me to tell my XO to get his ass in gear, or he personally would talk to my CO.

I approached the XO and politely told him a neighboring CO thought I should have been promoted by now. Nothing about getting his ass in gear. I was upset, but not yet suicidal.

He said the directive had come in some six weeks ago. "You should read the mail, Schick." Asshole.

About the same time a new ensign reported aboard for duty. A new supply and commissary officer. Yahoo!

I became a LTJG and electrical officer about the same time. Double promotion.

Qualification Texas-style

After reporting to his first submarine, an officer was given a year to "qualify." This involved learning the jobs of all the officers and enlisted men. It also meant tracing out and memorizing all the ship's systems: electrical, hydraulic, mechanical, radios, sonars, radars, torpedo tubes, main motors, generators, main engines, air compressors, bilge pumps, batteries, and so forth. It involved learning how to dive the boat under emergencies, how to fight fire, how to use the periscope and other sensors, and how to make ready and fire a torpedo. We kept a four-inch notebook, organized into sections. When we had completed a section, we would have a qualified officer walk us through it and ask questions until he was satisfied and signed us off.

In the process, we crawled through the bilges tracing electrical and hydraulic lines, spent hours memorizing communications procedures, begged the enginemen to let us start the engines, and generally worked our asses off. We even had to trace out the freshwater system to our sinks.

When all the sections had been signed, off the captain took you through your final onboard exam. There were no rules. He could ask any question or ask you to demonstrate your proficiency at any task. When he was satisfied he wrote a letter to the squadron recommending that you be designated "qualified in submarines." The squadron commander appointed another boat to administer your in-port exam, and you delivered your notebook to that skipper. After he had quizzed you and was satisfied, a third skipper was designated to administer an underway exam. On the appointed day that boat put to sea for the sole purpose of examining the candidate. Submariners put a lot of faith in this process. Gaining entry to the club was not taken lightly.

After a successful underway examination, the candidate reported to the division commander for his final oral exam. The divcom was not going to override three of his skippers so this was mostly an informal, congratulatory interview. After he signed off, you were a member of the club and pinned on your gold dolphins.

You could pin your dolphins on immediately but were expected to throw a qualification party for the wardroom in the reasonable future. At the party you would "drink your dolphins." This practice has been outlawed now. The politically correct pussies of the world have prevailed.

When the time came, late into the party, you were ready to drink your dolphins. The wardroom mixed a large drink—combining anything they could find in your liquor cabinet. They dropped your dolphins into the glass, and you chug-a-lugged, all in one deep drink, caught the dolphins in your teeth, and the skipper ceremoniously pinned them on.

We had a LTJG from Texas. Big guy. Big heart. He qualified, and the requisite party was scheduled. Great time. Lots of food, booze, and camaraderie. Came time to drink the dolphins. Big drink. Texas size. Down the hatch. No coming up for air halfway through. After all, this guy is not only a qualified submariner and a trained killer, he's a Texan.

Party goes on for a while and starts to die. Time to go home. All the coats had been piled on a bed. Somebody's wife goes in to the bedroom to retrieve her coat. Comes out of the bedroom screaming and laughing. Everyone rushes into said bedroom.

On top of the pile of coats on the bed is a stark naked, sound asleep Texas submariner smiling sweetly with his dolphins clutched in his hand.

Texas Fire Drill

Same Texas maverick. At this point, he is the engineer. The engineer, among other things, is responsible for damage control. That means leaks, fires, lost hydraulics, whatever.

We've been at sea for some time. Engineer is in his bunk, catching a few Zs. Skipper decides to have an unannounced fire drill. Takes a smoke canister, puts it in a waste can, pops the top, and shoves it into the engineer's stateroom. Smoke billows.

Engineer awakes, gets up, grabs the waste can, walks next door and puts the whole works in the skipper's stateroom, looks at the skipper and asks, "Did you lose this?" and goes back to bed. What a set of balls. Skipper laughing so hard we thought he'd have a heart attack. Good skipper, good engineer, good lessons for a young junior officer.

Mediterranean Cruise

After leaving the shipyard, *Irex* underwent a period of intensive training in preparation for a four-month deployment to the Mediterranean. While hard on the wives and families, extended operations at sea were the lifeblood of sailors. After all, most of us had joined the navy to see the world.

Getting ready to go was exciting. We took on extra spare parts and a full war-load of torpedoes. We loaded cases and cases of consumables. I had never seen so much toilet paper in one place. And we loaded food. Packed the walk-in freezer to the roof, stored thousands of eggs between the torpedo tubes, and even hung bags of onions and cabbages from the overhead pipes. Filled the enlisted shower with potatoes. We looked and smelled like an open-air produce market.

When all was ready, off we went. All the brass were on the pier to see us off and declare they wished they could be going, too. There was a small band to play martial tunes and a bunch of mournful wives trying to look brave. After we cleared the pier, Pat and the baby raced the car out to the Eastern Point Coast Guard Station, a rocky outcropping where the Thames enters Long Island Sound. They sat and watched us sail into the sound en route the Atlantic. Leaving her alone in Newport had been good training, and now she had John for company.

Learning Leadership

Our captain was the senior skipper on the river. As such, he did pretty much what he wanted. We called him the Great White Bellowing Whale—behind his back, of course. He had been around awhile and knew how to look after his crew. As officers, we had been taught that responsibility for the troops' well-being was our *first* responsibility. The skipper had done some planning along those lines before we ever left port.

Freshwater was always at a premium on a diesel boat. We carried a couple thousand gallons, which we took on from shore. But after we were at sea we had to make our freshwater from seawater, a laborious process. Freshwater was needed primarily for the engines and batteries, and only secondarily for cooking and washing.

We had a huge, specialized ballast tank called Safety Tank. Unlike the other ballast tanks, it was normally full of water whether on the surface or submerged. If the boat started to sink due to some emergency, it could be blown dry with compressed air, helping to get us back up on the surface. Now, here comes the leadership lesson.

Before we left port, the skipper had some rudimentary plumbing connected to Safety Tank. It involved installing a shower head up in the sail. Then he blew Safety Tank dry of saltwater and refilled it with freshwater from the pier. Voila! A 4,000-gallon freshwater tank for the crew's showers. While sailors on other submarines were jumping over the side, lathering up with saltwater soap, and jumping back in the ocean to rinse off (a less than optimum way to bathe), our guys were luxuriating in the freshwater shower from Safety Tank. Washing the salt off, even with cold water, made a big difference.

Meals at sea can get monotonous, particularly after the fresh food gives way to frozen, canned, and dried. A salad or a glass of fresh milk becomes only a distant dream.

A week or so after we had been at sea we were made aware of the reason we had "wasted" storage space for bags of charcoal. The skipper had caused a barbecue pit to be installed topside. On the forward deck, one could lift a hinged section of decking, and there was a gleaming, new, stainless steel BBQ pit, ready to be fired up.

Swim Call, Steaks, and Skeet

Monotony at sea is always a problem. There is an old saying that "life at sea consists of hours of boredom punctuated by moments of sheer terror."

So Skipper stops the ship.

Man on the bridge with an M-1 rifle to ward off sharks.

Sailors over the side to swim.

Cooks topside with the steaks.

Sailors back aboard to wash down with the freshwater from Safety Tank.

Charcoal-broiled steaks in the middle of the Atlantic.

Talk about a morale boost!

Again, we lie to (stop). Skipper is on the bridge. He sends below for the senior torpedoman. Gives him some quiet instructions, and the chief lays below.

A few minutes later, the chief and a couple of his troops arrive back topside lugging a shotgun, a tommy-gun, a bunch of ammunition, and some clay pigeons. They go out on deck and set up a skeet trap. The old man has done it again. The crew is invited topside to either shoot skeet or fire a Thompson submachine gun. Now we know why we loaded a double allowance of small arms ammunition.

Nowhere in navy regulations are freshwater conversions of Safety Tanks, BBQ pits, or skeet ranges mentioned. He took bold, unorthodox measures to ease the lives of his troops.

That's leadership.

More of the Same

One day, just before evening meal, the XO showed up in white tie and tails, complete with a gold-headed cane and a top hat. As he strolled jauntily through the boat, he stopped to chat with the crew, inquiring after their health, morale, and so forth. They thought he had lost it, but he sure gave them something to talk about for a while.

A few days later, we were sailing into a fifteen-knot wind. Beautiful day. Little popcorn clouds. Making twelve knots. 15+12=27 knots of wind blowing across the deck. CO is on the bridge taking in the fresh sea air. XO goes to the bridge carrying a mysterious sack. Word comes across the 1-MC (the general announcing loudspeaker system): "Anyone desiring to fly a kite, lay to the bridge. No more than two men at a time. Line forms below decks." The CO and the XO, like two twelve-year-old kids, are up on the bridge of a multimillion dollar, black, menacing, man-of-war, loaded with lethal torpedoes . . . flying kites. Forty or so sailors, little boys in grown men's bodies, are waiting patiently below decks to go up for a ten-minute turn.

Shipmates from the Past

After passing through the Straits of Gibraltar, we proceeded to the fleet anchorage off Spain. There were dozens of ships at anchor. One was the supply ship to which Ensign Stokes had transferred from *Gainard*. I got on the signal light and asked if he was aboard. She flashed back that LTJG Stokes was indeed aboard. I asked if she could send a boat over, and she did.

LTJG Stokes met me on the quarterdeck. He asked me if I'd like a tour of the ship. Topside was a mass of huge cranes, gantries, and other stuff I couldn't even name. It was fascinating. He introduced me to his number two, a warrant bo'sun who had been in the navy since Christ was a mess-cook. Certainly longer than I had been alive. Stokes said, "Boats, this is the man who taught me everything I know." I thought the bo'sun would pee his pants, he laughed so hard. Stokes only smiled.

Waterskiing

Enter Tracy Monroe Kosoff. When I reported to *Irex* as eleventh officer, Tracy was tenth. He was a 1958 graduate of the Academy—a classmate of Senator John McCain. Kosoff's hair became prematurely white at the age of seventeen. He was stocky, kinda like a fireplug. We nicknamed him Blaster, as in sandblaster, because he was built so close to the ground he blew sand around whenever he farted.

We were active water-skiers at the time. A fellow officer had a ski boat, and we spent many wonderful hours punishing our bodies on and in the Thames. A boat does not have to go really fast to pull a skier. Ten knots is enough. *Irex* could do twenty-seven knots on the surface.

As we were loading out to go to the Med, Tracy asked the skipper if we could take water skis with us. The CO laughed and said OK.

We made a 200-foot tow rope and loaded it and a pair of skis into an empty torpedo tube, there to be forgotten by all but the faithful.

After we had been in the Mediterranean for a while, we were scheduled to make a port call in Livorno, Italy. We had authorization to enter port at noon. We arrived early and were cruising slowly off shore waiting for the appointed time to enter port. Dozens of pleasure boats came out to see this sinister, black, menacing submarine. Some of the women on board these little boats were naked on top. Wow! In the early 1960s? How you gonna keep a boy down on the farm, once he has seen those large Italian tits? To hell with the hairy armpits.

Skipper's on the bridge, enjoying the scenery. Drinking coffee. Tracy and I go to the bridge. Tracy says, "Hey, Captain, may Bruce and I waterski?" CO says, "Sure. Where are your skis?" He had completely forgotten.

Down to the forward torpedo room. Open the tube. Out with the skis and tow rope. On with bathing suits and life jackets. Back to the bridge.

Skipper couldn't back down. Matter of honor. So he ordered all four engines on the line. Tracy first; he was senior. Take the slack out of the line. Now . . . all ahead full. Look, Ma, I'm skiing behind a submarine! The half-naked ladies went wild.

That evening, Tracy and I went ashore in our sparkling short-sleeve white uniforms. Couldn't buy a drink. In every bar we were recognized as the submarine skiers.

The nuclear navy killed all this kind of skylarking, but we had our day.

President Kennedy's Own

On a more serious note, this was the height of the Cold War. We had not been sent to the Med to waterski.

The Army Green Berets, an elite force that was the darling of President Kennedy, was a semi-secret organization of some of the toughest men in the world. The United States had recruited behind the Iron Curtain to find men whose families had been eliminated by the Communists. They were formed into small, self-sufficient units of totally dedicated professional killers, each with a large chip on his shoulder.

We took an A-Team on board: two officers and twelve men. The officers were American, but most of the troops barely spoke English. All they wanted to do was kill Commies.

We practiced surfacing, inflating their rubber boats, and sending them ashore. In Sicily, home of the Mafia. Somehow that seemed appropriate. Then we practiced picking them up. They would stretch a rope between their boats and bang on a piece of metal held underwater. We could hear them on our sonar and would try to hook the rope with a periscope. Then we would tow them offshore until it was safe to surface and take them back aboard. Neat stuff. This was real world. No playing around. Kill a Commie for Mommy.

Tracy and I begged to be allowed to ride with them one night. Each of us got his chance. After seeing how these guys operated, we were glad to be in the safety of a submarine.

Thank you, President Kennedy . . . and John Wayne. These troops later evolved into the Special Forces of the Vietnam era.

Royal Blue Suit

This skipper, with all his good points, was nonetheless human. Like all of us, he had his weaknesses. Among them was the unarguable fact he was tight as a drum. Still had the first nickel he ever made.

We made port in Naples. All sorts of hucksters lined up for their share of our good old American greenbacks. The skipper needed a new set of blues. Invited a Chinese tailor on board. Straight from Hong Kong. In *Naples!*

The tailor had all kinds of samples. Worsted, twill, flannel, etc. The skipper made his choice in the wardroom under fluorescent lights. Somebody said he ought to take that cloth up on the pier to view it in daylight. Not Barney! (Note: Like Skippsie, this was a nickname we did not use to his face.)

In a few days, maybe two, the new uniform arrived. Fit like a glove. Tailor-made. Looked great in the wardroom. Good price. Much cheaper than in the uniform shop in New London.

Out on the town. Wear the new splendor. Sunlight. The new uniform was bright blue. Not navy blue. Royal blue. Not even as subdued as Coast Guard blue. Nobody laughed to his face. After all, he was master after God. He wore it until he left *Irex* and defied anybody to challenge him. Big balls, tight purse. Prerogatives of command.

Full Coffee Cups

Diesel boats spent a lot of time surfaced, unlike nuclear boats which are designed to operate almost entirely submerged. The officer of the deck (OD) stood his watch on the bridge and was in charge of the entire ship. Four decks down, in the control room, the chief of the watch was in charge of all things below decks. The chief had large latitude in supervising normal housekeeping tasks. He could authorize anything on his own except a violation of hull integrity, that is, opening a valve that connected directly to sea. An example would be blowing sewage or garbage overboard.

All naval vessels run on gallons of strong coffee. When the OD and his two lookouts were in need, the OD would call down to the chief on the intercom (7MC circuit), "Control, bridge. One black and bitter, one black and sweet, and a blond and sweet to the bridge, please."

The chief would call the galley on the sound-powered phones and place the order. A mess cook would then carry the three steaming cups up four flights of vertical ladders—no mean feat. If only the OD wanted coffee, the chief would order it from the wardroom rather than the crew's mess. In this case, a steward rather than a mess cook would do the honors. In those days, most of the stewards were Filipinos. Sorry to be politically incorrect, but that was the way it was.

Most of the stewards had Spanish surnames. Read your history to find out why. We had one we'll call Gonzales, not his real name. In a particularly rough sea, he arrived on the bridge with two cups, one for the skipper and one for the OD. Both were full to the brim. The skipper asked him how he could climb four, ten-foot ladders in a rolling, pitching submarine without spilling a drop. He demonstrated proudly. He took a big drink from each cup to lower the level below the lip, held the coffee in his mouth until he was just below the bridge level, and spit it back into the cups. No spillage. He was so proud! He had little or no education, but he had solved a difficult fluid mechanics problem.

A side note on Filipinos in the navy. Living conditions in the Philippines were extremely poor. The U.S. Navy needed stewards, and most white sailors were unwilling to serve in what they saw as a demeaning role—waiting on officers. So an agreement was reached whereby Filipinos could serve as stewards while retaining their Philippine citizenship. As non-U.S. citizens, they paid no income tax. After serving twenty years, they were granted automatic U.S. citizenship, retired back to the Philippines, and paid no taxes there because now they were U.S. citizens. There was an annual enlistment quota and a long waiting list. A retired chief steward in Manila lived like a king. So much for exploitation.

Rota

The Med cruise was over, and it was time to head home. We stopped in Rota, Spain, to refuel. It would take about eight hours. The wardroom headed for the officers' club. It was ten o'clock in the morning, but we prevailed on the manager to open the bar. Started playing Liars' Dice. This is a game similar to poker, played with five dice. The object is to bluff. Part of the fun is cheating. We were playing for a quarter a game. The loser put a quarter in a glass to contribute to the next round of drinks. Big stakes.

Tracy and I, sitting at one end of the group, noticed that the CO and XO, sitting at the other, were cheating. They were rigging the game so that either Tracy or I, the two lowest-paid in the group, would lose. Never loath to be loud and disrespectful, we met the problem head on and confronted our tormentors. And were promptly thrown out of the game. Rank hath its privileges.

We retired to a nearby table and maintained our rate of alcoholic consumption. Presently, it was time to return to the boat. The skipper had a car and graciously offered us a ride with the rest of the officers. We, men of principle, declared we did not associate with cheaters. The fact that we had been cheating before we caught the other two had no bearing on the problem. In fact, we were better cheaters because we had not been caught.

Soon a pickup truck arrived with one of Tracy's sailors driving. He convinced us to ride back to the boat with him.

Underway for New London!

Soon after a submarine gets underway, it is "rigged for dive." This entails realigning many valves, which had been shut for safety in port, to a condition allowing the boat to submerge. Each compartment is rigged by a qualified enlisted man and then double-checked by an officer. The ship's diving officer, a collateral duty of the engineer, assigns officers to inspect specific compartments.

As we were proceeding briskly westward, the word came over the 1MC (public address system). "Lieutenants Schick and Kosoff report to the CO's cabin. Engineer, get a sober officer to check the engine rooms and After Battery rigged for dive." These were the compartments Tracy and I had checked. Somebody had ratted on us.

We reported as ordered. Skipper said, "Go get your swords." This was serious. We had both been in hack before, but swords? Admiral Nelson? Wow!

Back with the swords. Hand them over. We were in hack indefinitely. Confined to our cabins except to stand watch and use the head. Our meals would be served in our rooms. We were not fit to break bread with the other officers.

Riding the Snorkel

Submarines going from point to point submit a "movement report" to higher authority. They then transit in a ten by twenty-mile moving box called a "moving haven." If someone reports sighting an unidentified submarine, the same higher authority can determine if it is one of ours, and who. It was this skipper's custom to race to the front of the box and stop to play until we had drifted to the back of the moving box. At twelve-knots speed of advance (SOA), we could play about two hours.

The old man decided he wanted some photos of the boat submerging. We raced to the front of the box. It seemed to him that a good way to get pictures was to put two officers on top of the snorkel mast with a camera, raise the mast, and submerge. And he had two officers in hack. Prime candidates.

Tracy and I donned bathing suits and life jackets and climbed to the top of the mast, which was then raised. This put us about sixty feet above the surface of the ocean. One of us faced forward to take pictures of the bow going under, and the other faced aft. The good old beer can antenna was between our legs, so the aft-facing officer had only to put his arms around the other, and we were secure. When all was ready the boat submerged. Great fun!

Up came the periscope, ten feet in front of us. We were at a shallow depth, and our feet were three feet out of the water. The periscope was inspecting our feet. Oh, oh. The diving officer inched the boat deeper until the water was lapping at our toes. We scrunched our legs up onto the top of the snorkel valve, our knees tucked against our chests. Boat inched deeper. Damn!

On top of the snorkel valve is a little mechanical indicator that can be seen through the scope. It looks like a golf ball on a stick. When the valve is shut, the ball is snug against the top of the valve housing. When the valve opens, the ball pops up six inches or so. The conning officer can look through the scope and tell if the valve is open or shut. We were running with it shut, the little golf ball snug against the top of the valve. The diving officer can open the valve manually, which he now did. Little old golf ball popped up six inches on its stem. The bastard was trying to goose us! Valve shut, ball retracted. Valve opened, ball extended. Valve shut, etc.

After what seemed an eternity, the old man having had his fun, we surfaced. Good break in the monotony.

Needle

I had chronic problems with muscle spasms in my lower back. We slept on very thin mattresses over flimsy wire springs. The whole bed tended to sag like a hammock. I was advised to get a thick piece of plywood and insert it between my mattress and spring to provide some support. It helped a lot. And provided me a nickname.

Someone started the rumor that I had rolled over in bed while experiencing a nocturnal erection and gotten splinters from the bedboard in my penis. Occasion for a nickname! I was now "Splinterdick." But only briefly. That quickly changed to Needledick. And that to "Needledick the Bug Fucker." Our wardroom were an imaginative lot. The nickname stuck but was usually shortened to just plain Needle. The skipper often introduced Tracy and me to strangers as Blaster and Needle.

Silver Nitrate

Remember having to replace water in your car battery every so often before the days of so-called freedom batteries? We had to water batteries every three days or so, and it took as much as 700 gallons. The water had to be very pure. One of the tests for salinity was to mix a few drops of silver nitrate in a glass of battery water. If there was any salt in the water it would turn milky.

Silver nitrate was used in the medical profession to stop bleeding. Dentists were particularly fond of swabbing it on bleeding gums after an extraction. It turns skin black and cannot be washed off. It was also dropped into newborn babies' eyes to kill syphilis.

The skipper was bored again. We were three days out of New London, and everybody was at wit's end. Hadn't seen Mama for four months. I was summoned from my cabin to the wardroom. When I arrived, I was attacked and pinned to a bench seat. My shirt and T-shirt were ripped off. A wildly grinning CO began to paint lewd expressions on my belly with a Q-tip dipped in silver nitrate. In all honesty, I must admit this was a retaliatory payback. Earlier, when someone pointed out he was missing a button on his shirt, he looked down but couldn't find where one was gone. I obligingly ripped his shirt off so he could see it more clearly.

Here we were, a couple of days from home, having been gone four months, and my chest and stomach were covered with indelible obscenities. I was still in hack, and the skipper was noncommittal about letting me off when we made port.

In those days, each steward "adopted" a couple of officers. This was done informally and entirely on his own. As we prepared to enter port, "your" steward would break out a dress uniform, rig it (shine brass, attach ribbons, shoulder boards, and dolphins—if you were qualified in submarines), and brush all the lint away. He would also spit shine a pair of dress shoes. The stewards took great pride in "their" officers and competed to make them look their best.

Tracy and I told our stewards not to waste time on us as we were probably not going ashore for awhile. As we were entering Long Island Sound, the CO told the lead steward to have our gear rigged. *We were off the hook!* Those returned swords were a welcome sight.

We would be alongside for a month or so, and the CO declared a period of "basket leave." That meant officers and crew alike came in to work only on their duty days. Other mornings you just called in to telephone muster. The days off were not counted towards the thirty days of formal leave accrued each year.

It was great to be home!

Qualification Training

I had been procrastinating long enough, and it was time to finish up quals. Tracy qualified shortly after we returned to New London. I was next in line. The crew had been excellent teachers, and I was proficient, but was lazy about finishing my notebook. A short example of the quality of our sailors who taught us:

We had a second class electrician's mate named Petronzio. Like many of our sailors, he was from New England, educated in parochial schools by strict nuns. He was an expert operating the main propulsion cubicle. The cubicle was a large array of switches, gauges, rheostats, and other paraphernalia that controlled the speed and direction of the propellers. Ours was a split cubicle with one side for the port shaft, the other for the starboard. The electricians on watch controlled the main motors that turned the shafts, the generators or batteries which powered the motors, and the diesel engines. Before qualifying, an officer had to be able to operate the cubicle. Pete Petronzio was my instructor. He would stand behind me with an eighteen-inch ruler in hand. If I reached for a handle or wheel out of sequence or failed to decrease an amperage before I increased a voltage, *crack!* Down came the ruler on my wrist. In the regular navy this would be construed as an enlisted man assaulting an officer. Court-martial. In submarines, it was an expert teaching a neophyte. Many a nun must have smiled down from heaven to see Pete perform. Here again was a man with little formal education, but a great heart. By the time he was done with me, I was as good as any electrician.

Pete wanted to go back to Rhode Island and buy a chicken farm after he retired. I hope he did. The chickens would be well served.

A Fly in the Ointment

About this time I was ordered to go to Washington to be interviewed by Admiral Rickover for the nuclear power program. We were launching new nuclear submarines at a great rate, and there was a tremendous need for personnel to man them. The interview was voluntary, and I was not inclined to go. I was on the brink of qualifying and looking forward to life as a real submariner, not an unqualified puke.

I was summoned to the squadron commander's office for some very senior counseling. The commodore (courtesy title for squadron commander) informed me I was a volunteer for submarines, *all submarines,* and should I decline to submit to Rickover's interview, I was history in the submarine force. No-brainer. Off I went.

Rickover's offices were in the old Navy Annex, a relic of WWII. The entrance was in a back alley past a long row of garbage cans. He had been assigned these digs when he was a rebel captain and refused to relinquish them when he became successful. Now all comers from senators to midshipmen walked past the garbage, no pleasant undertaking in Washington's muggy summers. Revenge is so sweet.

There were twelve interviewees. We were given individual sessions with a couple of prospective commanding officers (PCOs) who were there for Rickover's six-month charm course. They were fair, strict, and very professional. Asked a lot of technical submarine questions. Then we were sequestered in a small room and told to stay there. The only reading materials were copies of the *Congressional Register* with Rickover's testimony highlighted.

As time passed, the call of nature increased, but we had been ordered not to leave the room under any circumstances. Finally, one of our number gave in and dashed down the hall to use the head. He never returned! A second soul succumbed to the call. He never returned!

The admiral's secretary's desk was positioned so she had a clear view of the door to the head. She had it timed perfectly. Just enough time to get the equipment out and begin relieving the pressure, when in the door she flew, grabbed the pisser by the arm, and dragged him, still dribbling, out of the head, across the hall, and into the admiral's presence. Still zipping up. She loved it. Bull dyke! I must have peed while someone else was interviewing, because I got safely back to the waiting room.

When I finally got in to see the old man I greeted him politely, "Good afternoon, Admiral." He replied, "I did not ask for a weather report." The interview went down hill from there. He asked where I had graduated in my academy class. I knew roughly, he knew exactly. He asked me why I stood higher my junior year than senior. I told him I had been dating seriously and paid less attention to my studies. He observed I had a child. I confirmed that, in fact, a second was on the way. Finally, he blew his cork.

"There are two kinds of officers in the navy: early birds and nest builders. You're a goddamn nest builder. Get out of my sight." End of interview. I was officially a "Rickover Reject" and happy to be so.

New London Shiphandlers

The New London submarine base is on the north bank of the Thames River. Landing a boat there was by far the most difficult shiphandling feat in the submarine force. The piers were built perpendicular to the river. Each pier could take a boat on both sides. This left about a boat's width between the two subs at adjoining piers. There was little room for error.

At this point in its rush to the sea, the Thames is tidal. On an outgoing tide, the current in the river would reach seven knots. And it ran at right angles to the piers. The formula to moor alongside was:

Go two piers up the river from the assigned berth.

Right full rudder. Port ahead full. Starboard back full.

This would put the boat in a full power twist to starboard.

As the boat twisted, it drifted downstream at seven knots.

When the boat was turned parallel to the piers:

All stop. Rudder amidships. Still drifting downstream.

When the bow was drifting past the assigned pier (if you were going portside to), or the submarine moored to your left (if going starboardside to the next pier downstream):

All ahead full.

Correct with the rudder.

When the front of the sail passed the end of the pier:

All stop. All back full.

Pray for the backing bell.

At the head of each pier was a pay telephone booth. Quite a few were taken out by colliding submarines. Next to the booth was the reserved parking spot for the CO. Couple of cars got taken out, too. Explaining to the insurance company that your car was run into by your submarine was a problem.

Qualification

Finally I was ready. The skipper signed me off. Took my inport exam on another boat with a neutral skipper. Ready for the big underway test. Remember the foregoing section on landing a boat alongside a pier in New London.

Irex had big, four-bladed screws. Lots of backing power. The boat I was going out on had newer, three-bladed screws. Quieter, but greatly reduced backing power, I was warned. No problem. I was twenty-four years old and a *New London boat driver.* I could thread a submarine through a keyhole.

(See previous sequence of commands.)

At the end, add "Oh shit!"

Scratch one phone booth.

An understanding skipper passed me anyway.

Interview with the division commander, largely ceremonial, and I was qualified in submarines! Pin on the Dolphins!

Chief Engineer

Shortly after I qualified, the engineer was commandeered for nuclear power training rather suddenly. Overnight I was selected to replace him.

Qualified in submarines! Chief engineer on a diesel boat! Talk about hog heaven!

Every other engineer on the river was a full lieutenant. I was still a LTJG. The chief petty officers in the repair shops on the base loved me.

I was a mascot. Most of them were old enough to be my father. They really looked out for me and *Irex*. They wouldn't let me fail.

Summertime

Porgy and Bess. "Summertime, and the living is easy." Qualified in submarines. Chief engineer. Baby John coming on. New brother/sister on the way. Snug nest . . . Rickover was right, I'm a nest builder. Happy in my work.

Operating in Long Island Sound. Middle of the night. Messenger wakes me up. "Message for you, Mr. Schick." Momma and son doing fine. Initial the message and back to sleep. Easy birth for me.

Next morning we meet a tug off the sea buoy, and I hop over. Back to New London. Over to the hospital to meet Will. How did Pat get to the hospital last night?

She called Tracy's fiancée, who called her father, who drove her to the hospital. He wasn't even navy, he just lived in a seagoing town.

And now we were four.

An old Navy saying. "You got to be there to lay the keel, but no need to be present for the launching."

My better half often reminded me we got back from the Med trip November 22, 1961. Will was born August 22, 1962. Quick work!

The Skipper's Complaints

The captain *loved* to write letters to higher authorities, jerking their chains. A couple of examples follow:

The Missing Diesel Fuel: The ship had to submit a quarterly fuel report to Washington, probably the Bureau of Ships (BUSHIPS). It was a very cumbersome form and seemed to us to be totally without merit. It took hours to fill it out. It contained gallons on board, gallons taken on during the quarter, sources of refueling, miles steamed, and Lord knows what additional garbage.

We received a nastygram from some desk jockey at BUSHIPS returning our report and pointing out that there was a discrepancy of some 100 gallons. Our fuel capacity was some 200,000 gallons. To anyone with a brain, there had been an obvious arithmetical error. A simple correction would have been the normal reaction, along with some bitching about BUSHIPS bureaucrats. But our skipper could not pass up the chance to tweak the tiger's tail. He drafted, with much glee, a long letter in which he explained that:

1. He had a deep appreciation of the value of our diesel oil as a part of the navy's overall consumption.

2. As a consequence, he had organized the crew into search parties, sounded all the fuel tanks, and searched the bilges.

3. The crew had found the errant 100 gallons in the Forward Engine Room bilge.

4. Unfortunately, the sailors were so dirty from their search efforts they had used the diesel to remove the grease from their clothes and bodies, and it could not be returned to storage.

5. In order to keep the records straight, he was enclosing his personal check in the amount of $12.00, the prevailing price for 100 gallons of navy diesel fuel.

He fired the letter off to Washington and never got an answer, but somebody had the balls to cash his check.

The Green Weenies: Submarines got the large bulk of their food from normal navy supply channels. There was an exception, however. If an item was not available in the supply system, we could purchase it at the base commissary. We routinely used to get extra goodies this way. Among them were first-rate hot dogs.

But hot dogs were also available in the navy system, and somebody reviewed our open-purchase (commissary) records and sent another nastygram demanding an explanation.

Now the navy-issue dog was about 80 percent cereal, 10 percent meat, and 10 percent fat. The crew wouldn't eat them. Moreover, they often turned a mottled green when boiled, making them even more unattractive. And they smelled awful.

Time for another letter to Washington. The CO reported he had conducted a scientific study (he always did so for one of his letters) and found that nothing helped the palatability of the green weenies. He had fried them whole, sliced and fried them, boiled them, baked them, and simmered them in baked beans, all to no avail.

Bingo! We got a letter back authorizing us to buy franks on the open market until the navy food folks could conduct their own study. The Old Man was ecstatic. *He had beaten the system.*

The Urinals: We received a directive, complete with blueprints, to lower the height of the urinals. Apparently some vertically challenged sailor couldn't get it over the edge (this before the days of women on ships). Repair funds were always tight, and the Old Man felt this was not a good use of his allotted dollars. Time for another letter.

After another intensive study, he reported that he had observed the entire crew in action at the existing urinals and only a few had difficulty getting over the edge. This had been solved by training them to "reel out more hose."

Never got an answer to this one either, but he never refurbished the pissoirs.

Practical Jokes

Sailors love practical jokes like babies love ice cream. Just two here by way of illustration:

Blowing the After Battery Head: A diesel submarine had three heads, one each in the Forward and After Torpedo rooms, and one in the After Battery compartment. The After Battery also contained a large sleeping area, the mess decks, and the galley.

Commodes were flushed with a small amount of seawater into a holding tank called, somewhat amusingly, Sanitary Tank. When the tank was full, the contents were blown overboard with compressed air. Blowing Sanitary was a delicate task because if not done just right, the sewage blew back into the boat and all over the sailor doing the blowing. The After Battery Sanitary was normally blown by a mess cook who was already on duty in the galley. The duty cook would call the diving officer on the phone to get permission. If any problem arose, the auxiliaryman-of-the-watch would be dispatched to assist. He was an engineman or machinist mate and had better knowledge of valves and pipes than a mess cook. Needless to say, the auxiliarymen were never amused to be summoned.

One day permission was requested and granted to blow the After Battery Sanitary Tank. Shortly thereafter, trouble was reported and the auxiliaryman dispatched. Grumbling, he headed aft. On arrival, he found shit and toilet paper all over the place. The cursing could be heard two compartments away.

The cook quietly scraped a two-finger glob of peanut butter from a nearby jar and ambled back to the head. Arriving on scene, he asked the auxiliaryman what the problem was. The answer was immediate and furious. "Your #@*?# mess cook has blown shit all over the place."

The cook reached up to the overhead (ceiling), scraped off a glob of peanut butter, which he had kept concealed in his hand, tasted it, and reported, "Yep. That's shit." The auxiliaryman promptly puked.

The Submarine Pain Test: Each of the engine rooms contained a large steel workbench with a sturdy vise affixed to it. These were sometimes used to administer the Submarine Pain Test to new, unsuspecting victims.

When an innocent patsy decided to take a stroll aft, word would be passed via the sound-powered phones to one of the engine rooms. Each engine room was manned by a senior throttleman and an oiler. When the pigeon arrived, the oiler would have the tips of both index fingers inserted in the vise, and the throttleman would be cranking down on the handle. Naturally, our novice would ask what was going on. He would be told he was witnessing the Submarine Pain Test, a measure of a man's ability to endure the hardships of life at sea. Almost always he immediately pleaded to take the test. Normally, the throttleman would say the volunteer was too new on board, too young, too frail, etc. Reeling in the fish was half the fun. Finally relenting, he would allow our young choir boy to insert his digits. Cranking the vise tightly on the proffered joints affected immediate and complete capture.

Quickly the lad's pants were lowered and a grease gun stuck up his ass to give him a liberal dose. He was then released and congratulated on passing the infamous Submarine Pain Rest. Sailors are easily amused.

The Submarine Birthday Ball

The Birthday Ball was a big deal. We were all very proud, and this was the big party of the year. The admiral came up from Norfolk, we all dressed up in mess-dress uniforms, and the wives donned gowns. Most navy wives were very attractive. Why not? They were married to us. And low-cut gowns were popular. If you've got it, flaunt it.

The ball sparkled. The women were beautiful, the officers handsome. Wine flowed freely. One of our *Irex* wives leaned too far over the table and . . . well . . . her tit fell out of her gown. Sitting out there in front of God and everybody. Handsome thing. She was unaware of her predicament. Our gallant Tracy Kosoff, Officer and Gentleman by Act of Congress, leapt to the rescue. Picking up a soup spoon, he delicately shoehorned the exposed breast back into the nest from which it had escaped. What charm! What quick thinking!

Her husband, observing the rescue, commented languidly, "Hey, Blaster. Couldn't you have heated that spoon up a bit? Lillian doesn't like cold hands." Oh, to be young again.

The Brink

We got a new skipper. Tracy left for duty at the Squadron. Life in the peacetime navy was good. Then the headlines screamed. The Soviets were sending missiles to Cuba. President Kennedy stood up to the threat. Nikita Kruschev refused to back down. The world teetered on the brink of a nuclear crisis.

We went on alert and prepared to go to sea. The piers were a madhouse. Long lines of torpedo dollies waited to unload their deadly cargo. We took on a full ninety day load of food. Workers arrived and welded all but the conning tower hatches shut so they could not blow open if we were depth charged. TOP SECRET orders arrived, to be opened only after we put to sea. The daily press reports escalated. The crisis deepened. We were truly scared.

We knew that in the event of nuclear war, I was safer than Pat and the kids. I would be at sea. They would be at New London, home of the U.S. Submarine Force—a sure target for the Soviets. What to do after the holocaust, if it happened? Her parents owned a cottage in New Hampshire, far from any military target. We agreed that if bad came to worse, she and the kids would try to get there. If I got back, that's where I would look for them.

This was no Cold War novel. This was real. Finally, all the boats were ready and we sortied en masse. 'Twas a fearful day. We had no idea what we would come home to if indeed we did return. As we (the diesel boats) passed State Pier where all the nucs were moored, we noted that none of them were preparing to get underway. Least of our concerns.

We went north to the Iceland-U.K. Gap. The gap was a natural bottleneck for Soviet ships steaming south. We formed an antisubmarine barrier. It consisted first of a line of P-3 sub-hunter aircraft. The next line was made up of destroyers. The idea was for the airplanes to locate ships and report to the destroyers, which would attack if ordered. We, as the principal antisubmarine weapons platforms, were in the third line. We would pick off any submarines or surface ships that got through the first two lines of defense.

In the beginning, the worst part was lack of news. We received a short news summary by radio broadcast every day but it was no substitute for the *Wall Street Journal*. We had little idea what was going on in the big picture. We were busy enough, however, listening on our sonars to the Russian warships and submarines streaming south.

Ready Warheads

Both torpedo rooms and all ten tubes were full. But the fish in the tubes were on "safe." That is, they had to be withdrawn and made fully ready before they could be fired. After we were well clear of port and on the high seas, the torpedo officer duly asked the CO for permission to make the tube-loaded fish fully ready. This procedure would take about four hours. After the torpedoes were ready, we could go to battle stations and fire in a few minutes.

The new CO, a liberal Yankee, refused permission. He would not be responsible for "Starting World War III." *We were sailing into the teeth of the Soviet navy with no bullets in our guns! Jesus H. Christ!* We were on station fifty-six days and never made a torpedo ready to fire. Had we been fired upon, we would have been totally defenseless. The skipper's decision bordered on criminal. Over a hundred lives were at stake.

Freshwater

A diesel submarine uses a lot of freshwater. It refills the main batteries, cools the main engines, cooks food and washes dishes, and, if there is any left, cleans the crew. We carried some from port, but then had to make it from seawater. Since we did not have steam boilers like a surface ship, we made it using compressor distillers. Our compressors were extremely noisy. Submarines are supposed to be very quiet, especially when there are a lot of bad guys around. So we ran the compressors as little as possible and only when we were snorkeling. To conserve water, each man was allowed one cup a day for hygienic purposes. Most of us used it in the morning to brush our teeth.

Obviously, there were no showers. Nor sponge baths. Body odor was no problem, as our sense of smell went dead after a week or so.

But then the green grungies started. Mold. Under our arms and in our crotches. Itchy. Luckily, our corpsman had anticipated this problem and purchased cases of those little bottles of Absorbine Jr. before we sailed. The ones with the sponge over the opening. Worked like a champ, but stung like hell. Armpits were a breeze, but we had to be awfully careful in the nether area.

We went fifty-three days without showers. And the president stared the Soviets down and averted WWIII. I'm still proud of my small part.

Last Comment

When we arrived back at New London and steamed up the Thames, the nucs were still moored alongside State Pier. They had been considered "too valuable to put at risk." So much for high-tech, expensive weapons. Our sailors literally waved handkerchiefs at the poor bastards as we passed close aboard. Wasn't their fault. I'm sure they were as eager as we to put to sea to defend the old USA. But in the eyes of the brass, we were expendable and they were not.

P.S.: Our arrival time was still secret. But Tracy was on the staff and leaked it to the wives so they could get their hair done or whatever. He also came down to the boat and took the duty for the OOD so he could go home. Thanks, Blaster.

DEPCOMSUBLANT

I had been in *Irex* four years and was overdue to rotate. I had come aboard as an ensign and eleventh officer; now I was a full lieutenant and third officer. I really liked being chief engineer and had arranged to go to the staff as a division engineer. At the last minute, I was asked if I was willing to be an admiral's aide instead. I accepted the offer, departed *Irex,* and reported to the staff of Deputy Commander, Submarine Force, U.S. Atlantic Fleet (DEPCOMSUBLANT) to be aide and flag lieutenant.

The Commander, Submarine Force, U.S. Atlantic Fleet (COMSUBLANT) is headquartered in Norfolk, Virginia. He reports to Commander in Chief, U.S. Atlantic Fleet (CINCLANTFLEET). As the name implies, he has overall responsibility for submarines in the Atlantic. His staff concentrates on operations, intelligence, and readiness.

The Deputy Commander, Submarine Force, U.S. Atlantic Fleet (DEPCOMSUBLANT) was headquartered in New London, Connecticut. He reported to COMSUBLANT. His staff was responsible for personnel and materiel.

There were one hundred officers on the staff and thirty or forty enlisted men, including fifteen stewards. As admiral's aide, I served as his personal attendant and ran the flag mess, to which the stewards were attached. As flag lieutenant, I was in charge of the admiral's barge, and his car and driver.

The Admiral

"My" admiral was Rear Admiral Vernon L. Lowrance of Winston-Salem, North Carolina, known to his peers as "Rebel." He was a Southern gentleman to the bone. He spoke slowly and with a deep Southern accent. He was unfailingly courteous and cared deeply for those under his command. He also wore four Navy Crosses. Two incidents illustrate his concern for his subordinates.

He came to DEPCOMSUBLANT from command of a cruiser by way of chief of naval intelligence. He brought with him his favorite steward, a second class petty officer, to serve in his quarters. He arranged for quarters on the base for his steward's family, and just before they arrived, the admiral personally stocked their refrigerator with food and decorated their kitchen with fresh flowers.

Later on, when his driver, a first class engineman, remarked in passing one morning that his washing machine had given up the ghost, the admiral decided that the one in his quarters was not big enough (for a family of two) and had it delivered to the driver's house. Not as a gift, mind you, but as "surplus."

What great examples of selfless compassion!

The Aide

I was fresh off a boat with grease still under my fingernails when I reported to the staff. I was an almost-new lieutenant, twenty-six years old, and gung-ho. I switched from rumpled khakis to dress blues, buckled on my sword when required, and became somewhat civilized under the gentle guidance of "my" admiral.

As a first order of business, the boss told me to "stay out of photographs." The mark of a good aide was to be invisible. He also cautioned me never to wear his stripes without his prior consent. An aide has a tremendous amount of reflected power. As a conduit to the admiral, he is constantly approached by those seeking access to the throne. Admiral Lowrance was well aware of the way things worked and was coaching me in a fatherly way. Mrs. Lowrance was equally kind and helpful.

He did not like to carry money. Periodically he would write me a check, and I would keep his petty cash in a cigar box. Whenever we went somewhere, I would pick up the tab with his money. When I ran low, he would write another check. He never asked for an accounting.

I kept his uniforms in order. I made sure they were clean and starched. I rigged his medals. I made sure his white gloves had no obvious holes.

I kept his social calendar (in close coordination with Mrs. Admiral). Every morning, the admiral's driver picked me up at home and we went to the admiral's quarters to pick him up.

Last, but not least, the Old Man periodically sent me down to the waterfront to see what was going on in the trenches. People would tell me stuff they would never tell him, but they knew I was a direct conduit to him. This was not spying, but rather his way of keeping his finger on the unofficial pulse. I used to attend Happy Hour at the Officers' Club regularly. Reduced price on drinks. He went so far as to ask if he could go along to be introduced to some of my *very junior* friends. He would sit happily sipping a beer and chatting with the young turks who would otherwise never get to converse with an admiral. He was expert at listening to their banter and obviously enjoyed the camaraderie. It provided valuable insights to him and was a great morale boost for them.

Hail and Farewell

It was customary to give a party for officers departing and those newly reported on board. These were called Hail and Farewells.

Shortly after arriving on the staff, we received an invitation to an H & F at the admiral's quarters. Dress was "casual." To us, casual was a sweatshirt and shorts. Luckily, someone told me "casual" meant you could wear a sport coat and tie instead of a suit.

We arrived at the appointed hour, appropriately dressed. Never saw so many captains in my life! Old guys—late thirties, early forties. I was scared to death.

Dinner was served at card tables. I was seated with the flag secretary (a full commander) and two older, well-groomed women. One was the chaplain's wife (he was a captain), and the other was the chief of staff's wife (also a captain). The dinner was elegant. Broiled chicken served on pineapple quarters with the leaves still attached. I was doing fine.

At one point, one of the ladies asked the other, "Aren't these yellow pear tomatoes in the salad just lovely?"

She replied, "I don't know. Bruce has eaten my salad." Great start.

After dinner, the gentlemen retired for brandy and cigars, while the ladies went upstairs to "powder their noses." I'm told a conversation ensued among the fairer sex about the relative merits of a garter belt versus a girdle to hold up one's stockings. Everyone wore girdles in those days, a carryover from the older corsets. One of the ladies exclaimed that Pat was young and would be in on the latest fashion, and proceeded to lift her skirt to see. Only to find she was wearing a garter belt *but no panties.*

Welcome to the big leagues.

Medals or Ribbons?

The admiral's presence at an official function was a big deal. If one was to be held on one of the boats or at the Officers' Club, I would go ahead of time to iron out the details. There were only a couple of basic rules: 1. No surprises, 2. Be in the proper uniform, and 3. Be exactly on time. Nothing could be worse than the boss arriving early before all the host players were in place. He also would have been upset to keep anyone waiting.

There was some kind of function scheduled in the base gymnasium, I can't recall what. There were to be several submarine crews in attendance. I did a routine precheck. No problems.

Prior to the event, I got out a clean, starched set of the admiral's dress whites and had a steward polish his white shoes and rig his uniform. "Rigging" a uniform consists of attaching shoulder boards if required, medals or ribbons, submarine and other insignia, and in the case of dress whites, removable buttons. Medals are the large metal medallions attached to colorful wisps of ribbon. They sway and clank. Ribbons are the less formal equivalent. They are merely 1 by ¼-inch pieces of ribbon of the same pattern as the parent medal.

Now remember, the admiral had earned four Navy Crosses. The Navy Cross is second only to the Medal of Honor, our country's highest award for military gallantry. *Both* of his sub school roommates had won *Medals of Honor*!

Steward pops his head in my office. "Medals or ribbons, Lieutenant?"

Distractedly, "Ribbons, please."

Wrong. Everybody else but me and the boss were tricked out in dangling, sparkling, clanking, *medals.* And not one Navy Cross in the whole lot.

After we got back to headquarters, he called me into his office and told me to sit down. I knew I was in trouble whenever he asked me to sit. He explained very quietly and slowly that even admirals were expected to be in proper uniform, and it was their aides' responsibility to make sure they were. Then he said, "No great harm done. Be more careful in the future." And that was the end of that.

Mrs. Admiral

The New London Submarine base is located on the site of an old farm. The old farmhouse, nicely renovated, served as the admiral's quarters. It was under the command of the admiral's wife, in this case one Claire Lowrance. Her only child, Doug, was also a submariner, two years my senior, and she treated me like a second son.

Mrs. Lowrance kept their social calendar, and I kept his official one. Every Wednesday morning I reported to the quarters, and we compared notes. She took advantage of these occasions to mine me for what was going on at the staff, where were the problems, and what the admiral was overlooking or where she needed to prod him gently. She was never intrusive, but those conversations gave me a back door to the boss. She also gave me invaluable advice, not only about my job, but sometimes how to get the admiral to do what she wanted. I have met few women whom I admire so much.

Hoses

The base commander, a captain, lived in the house next to the quarters. It was a nice house, but not as nice as the admiral's. The captain was a passed-over dead-ender. He would never make admiral, and he knew it. He was bitter and more than a little bit pompous. He was not popular with the troops or Mrs. Admiral. And he was a gardener. So was Mrs. Admiral.

There were no underground lawn sprinklers in those days. Garden hoses were the order of the day. Mrs. Lowrance, at her own expense, had bought several to water her lawn and gardens.

One day, the base commander, without permission, walked next door, unhooked the Lowrance's hoses, dragged them home, and hooked them up. Voila! Green lawn! Wrong!

The missus got an ax, walked next door, and severed all of her stolen hoses. Take that! Next time, ask first.

The White Couch

My in-laws were coming for a visit. They had never met an admiral. We got ourselves invited to the quarters on a Sunday afternoon so that the boss could meet his aide's relatives. Very kind of a busy man. At the last minute, the baby-sitter cancelled. Placed a phone call to cancel our visit. No way. The missus said bring the boys. We arrived. The admiral was charming . . . made the in-laws feel like members of the family. The stewards served cocktails. The missus insisted the boys have Oreos and milk. The boys were seated on a *white brocade couch.* God, what a mess.

Horses Sweat

One of the major duties of an aide, and his wife, is to help at official parties. The aide heads up the receiving line, collects names, and passes them up the line. The wife circulates and makes sure everybody is doing OK. Another one of her jobs is to rescue the admiral or his wife from bores who are dominating their time. The number of social-climbing, inconsiderate, loudmouthed individuals was astounding.

Midsummer. Unusually hot and humid. No air-conditioning at the quarters (not needed in New England). Very important party entertaining the civilian elite of greater New London—mayors, former mayors, wannabes and been-there-almosts. Hot as the hinges of hell. Herself is eight months pregnant. Looks like she swallowed a watermelon. Perspiring heavily. Suddenly feels a little light-headed. Sits down. I'm busy elsewhere. Admiral goes to the rescue. Somebody tells me my wife is sick. When I arrive on the scene, the boss is administering first aid (a cool glass of water).

I am supposed to be serving the admiral, not the reverse. I am embarrassed all to death, and tell him so. Worried about Pat sweating so much and say that, too. He smiles and says: "Horses sweat. Men perspire. Ladies glow."

No problem.

Stiff Collars

A new chief of staff was coming. The COS is the admiral's principal assistant. He is in charge of the day-to-day functioning of the staff, and more importantly, serves as the boss's primary advisor and confidant. As a result, he is generally handpicked by the admiral and is usually a close and trusted friend. Our new COS also had a reputation as being hard as nails and really tough to work for. We'll call him Pinky, for that was indeed his nickname.

Pinky reported aboard and quickly took charge. He was a no-nonsense guy of the old school. Very strict. There was some grumbling, but he was intelligent, dedicated, and fair. Folks soon adapted to his leadership style, but remained in absolute terror of him—I think he liked it that way.

Shortly after his arrival, he wandered into my office. I was working in shirtsleeves, my blouse neatly hanging on a coatrack. He poked around a bit and then remarked that I was wearing a "soft" collar—wash and wear shirts were all the rage at the time. When I allowed that was true, he informed me that *gentlemen* wore *starched* collars. Only low-lifes and pimps wore soft ones. I got the idea.

Dry Martinis

It was customary, when arriving at a new command, to pay a formal call on the skipper. He and his wife would return the call. With 100 officers on the staff, it was impractical to make and return individual calls, so the new chief of staff announced a series of "Calls Made and Returned" receptions at his quarters. About a quarter of the staff were invited to each. These mandatory calls served as both the officers' calls on the COS and his on them. He borrowed me from the admiral to arrange the functions and man the receiving line, make introductions, and manage the party. These were very formal, choker-white affairs. About a half-dozen stewards manned each, cooking, serving, and tending bar.

Martinis were the most popular drink in this pre-politically-correct pre-white-wine navy. Pinky instructed me ahead of time that he wanted *dry* martinis, 5 to 1, not 3 to 1. I dutifully passed his instructions on to the bartenders.

About a half hour into the party, the lead steward informed me they were running out of vermouth. We had a deal with the Officers' Club, whereby we could, in a pinch, borrow liquor from the bar and pay later. I sent one of the stewards to the club for a bottle of vermouth.

About another half hour later . . . same thing . . . running out of vermouth. Suddenly, I was aware of what was going on. The bartenders were mixing the martinis 5 to 1 as directed, only they were using five parts vermouth to one part gin. Oh my god!

After the party, I confessed to Pinky, fully expecting to be doused with the remaining gin, of which there was an abundance, and ignited. To my great surprise, he thought it was funny. "If those people are so afraid of me they will drink straight vermouth and not complain, I'll save a fortune on my entertaining bill" was all he said.

The Flag Suite

The bachelor officers' quarters had a small, attached wing called the flag suite. It consisted of four large, well-appointed bedrooms, a huge sitting room, a large dining room, and a kitchen. It was used to house visiting dignitaries. The BOQ officer-in-charge had no authority over it. It belonged to me. Aside from using it for visiting guests, the admiral also did quite a bit of official entertaining there. At the most elegant formal dinners, we literally had a white-gloved steward standing behind each diner throughout the meal. We had sent several stewards to train with the finest New York hotel chefs, and they prepared some pretty fancy meals. (By the way, the hotels donated these apprenticeships as a show of their respect for the military.) All in all, it was a holdover from the nineteenth century. It was here that I learned a bottle of port is never lifted from the tablecloth, but slid along on its bottom to the next person.

Toilet Paper

My admiral's boss was COMSUBLANT, a vice admiral in Norfolk. He frequently stayed in the flag suite. Before a visit, I would personally inspect to ensure his favorite snacks and drinks were available, his room was perfect, and so forth. A junior steward slept on a cot in the kitchen just in case he needed anything in the night.

One night in the wee hours, the telephone rang and a terrified duty steward said the Big Admiral wanted to see me at the flag Suite *now!* I jumped into some clothes and sped to the BOQ, where he met me at the door and escorted me into his bathroom.

"Feel that toilet paper!"

"Aye, aye, sir."

"Where did you get it?"

"Navy issue, sir."

"Well, you get your young ass out of here and find me some *soft* paper *now*!"

How was I to know he suffered from major hemorrhoids?

The Brits

The Royal Navy was coming to New London on a goodwill cruise. They were bringing a submarine tender, four or five boats, a rescue vessel, and a band. There was a flag embarked in the tender, and the first lord of the British admiralty would be joining us. What excitement!

A great gala was planned for the flag suite. We could seat only twenty or so in the dining room, so planning the guest list was a tough job. Mrs. Admiral came through as always. The reception was strictly stag. A long cocktail hour preceded dinner. Wines were served with each course, and port was passed after. Then all retired to the sitting room for brandy and cigars. Everyone was in a jovial mood.

The first lord, senior in the room, politely asked the admiral if the Yanks would be interested in playing a few friendly games. Of course the boss said yes.

Lord Jellico took charge immediately. He ordered his officers, including his admiral, to move all the furniture back against the walls. Then he had someone strip the sheets off a bed. They were quickly turned into a "rope." Then, stripping off his tuxedo jacket, cummerbund, tie, and shirt, he ordered his officers to strip for action, and they immediately shed their mess dress attire and stood ready. "We'll have a tug-of-war," said the most senior officer in the Royal Navy. "Prepare for action, Yanks." Whereupon, we shed our jackets, ties, and shirts.

"We'll compete sitting down," said his lordship, and we did. Rolling around on the dusty rug having a ball. Various games followed . . . arm wrestling, leg wrestling, plain wrestling, leapfrog, running the gauntlet. Had to send a steward to the Officers' Club for more booze. What a night! The Brits are great fun.

One More Brit Story

During their visit, the Brits did some entertaining of their own. Since the submarine tender was very large, and since the Royal Navy serves alcohol on board ship, they threw a big bash for all our officers and their wives. They also rented a big hall in town and threw a big party for the sailors. Classy.

We all gathered on the tender, dressed in our choker whites. Our ladies were resplendent in their party frocks. The sun was setting. Colors were retired. The band played on the pier. "God Save the Queen." "The Star Spangled Banner." We were comrades, separated only by a common language. Submariners!

The party ended too soon, and some of us, with our new British friends, proceeded to a private residence to continue the festivities.

Now the staff in the tender included a doctor. As I remember, he was a full commander. He attended the party dressed in a naval officer's blouse (jacket) and a kilt. This was a proper uniform. Late in the evening, some of the American wives became curious about the age-old question, "What does a Scotsman wear under his kilt?" Finally, one of them got up the nerve to ask. Our good doctor obligingly silenced the crowd, proceeded to the middle of the room, and executed a perfect handstand. *Voila! Nothing under his kilt!*

Tiptoe through the Tulips

In those days, we enjoyed a rich social life. Everyone entertained at home. Even if the pay was short, we managed to get together often with our friends. Maybe it was because we spent so much time at sea, separated from our loved ones. The Officers' Club was central to our lives. Baby-sitters were cheap, and so were food and drink at the club.

At the time, the base XO was a commander named Jim Bradley. Unlike the base CO, about whom you read earlier, the XO was a prince of a guy. He had come to New London from a tour as assistant naval attaché in Moscow. He would go on to become a legend in the submarine intelligence community.

One fine spring evening the missus and I, along with some other loyal patrons, closed the club at one o'clock or so. As we left she pointed out a beautiful bed of tulips in full bloom by the porch steps. They fairly glowed in the moonlight. Well, being an officer and a gentleman by act of Congress, I promptly dropped to my knees and began to gather a bouquet for my lady. Had picked a pretty good-sized bunch when I noticed a pair of shoes close aboard my starboard ear. Oh, oh! Looked up into the broadly grinning face of the base XO—the officer charged with maintaining good order and discipline on the base. I hadn't been in hack for over a year. What would the admiral say?

Still smiling, the XO leaned over and said, "Bruce. While you're down there, could you pick some for my wife, too?"

Years later, when I was a commander and working the intelligence game in Washington, I had the pleasure of doing business with this fine man. We both remembered fondly that night in the tulip bed. I sometimes wonder if this kind of camaraderie exists in the navy today. . . . I hope so.

Class Rings

In the early sixties all submariners, officer and enlisted, were volunteers. Most were career navy—in for twenty or thirty years. "Lifers." Most of the officers were Naval Academy alumni, called "ring knockers" for our out-sized class rings. The term was either pejorative or envious depending on your point of view.

Shortly after I was ordered to the staff I bought a new set of dress blues. My old ones smelled like diesel oil, and an admiral's aide has to set an example. I also bought a pair of shoes made from Corfam, a new kind of plastic stuff that gleamed like patent leather and never needed shining.

The boss and I were riding to New York for some fancy function. He looked over and said:

"New blues?"

"Yes, sir."

"Nice. New shoes, too?"

"Yes, sir."

"You look good, Bruce. How come you don't wear your ring?"

"Gained some weight, Admiral, and it's too tight."

"Take it to a jewelry store and have it enlarged. I wouldn't want people to think my aide was a ROTC. Charge it to me if you like."

I got the message. ROTC is the acronym for Reserve Officer Training Corps, the largest supplier of ensigns to the fleet. At the time of the conversation reported above, in the submarine force, you asked, "What class is he?" The assumption was that an officer was a graduate of Annapolis. Within a short time, the question became, "What year-group is he?" The admiral didn't have much use for reserves.

The Train

We had to go to the Philadelphia shipyard to inspect a boat. The admiral told me to call COMFAIRQUONSET to see if we could borrow his airplane. As a naval aviator, the admiral at Quonset had a plane assigned for his personal use. It was available and would pick us up at the little New London commercial airport.

At the appointed hour, off we went. In Philadelphia, a surprise snowstorm had arrived. The runway was dusted, and the wind was howling. The pilot made a very rough landing. Turns out he was a reservist on active-duty training and didn't have much experience in this type aircraft.

Not many people knew it, but the boss had gone to flight school right out of the academy. Unfortunately for naval aviation, but fortunately for the submarine force, he attempted a wheels-up landing at Pensacola. Landing, or more properly skidding with the landing gear still retracted into the fuselage, does not endear oneself with the naval aviation authorities, airplanes being rather expensive toys. Not to make too fine a point, but the admiral was a very nervous flier.

He told me to thank the pilot and send the aircraft back to Quonset Point. We would take the train home.

After the inspection, we were driven to the Thirtieth Street Station in what was by now a blizzard. Knowing that airlines would be grounded and the trains crowded, I had the staff at the shipyard obtain our tickets. Sure enough, trains were full and running late. We waited in the terminal for our train. The boss got hungry, looked around, and spotted a hot dog kiosk. Asked me to get us a couple of dogs and some Cokes. I carried the petty cash. But on this occasion, we were to have traveled solely by navy transport, and I had not brought any money. Had to borrow from His Nibs.

After a long, tedious, exhausting trip, we finally arrived in New London. It was the wee hours of the morning, and the blizzard was still raging. They had put a bunch of additional cars on the train to handle the overload, and when we swung down, we were a hundred yards up the track from the platform. Dead tired. Cold. Hungry.

As we trudged through the snow along the tracks, he said, "You know, Bruce, when I came to New London as an ensign, I had on a new set of blues. These are new. Not a dime in my pocket. Same as now, since I had to loan you my money for the hot dogs. But at least I had a bottle of whiskey in my pocket. Damn. I need a drink!"

Time To Move On

Good news! The boss was to get a third star and move to Norfolk as Commander, Submarine Force, Atlantic Fleet (COMSUBLANT). He asked if I would like to go along as his aide. I did not know the Norfolk area and thought a local officer could do a better job, so I respectfully declined. He told me his replacement was an SOB and I should move on, not stay as the new guy's aide. Where did I want to go? I had no idea. He said I ought to go to Defense Intelligence School. I opined that school requests had been due months ago, and we had missed the deadline by a mile. He smiled, made a phone call, and my orders arrived within a week. Off to D.C.

Fort Meade

The Naval Field Operations Intelligence Office (NFOIO) was a tenant activity at the National Security Agency, the nation's most secret eavesdropping entity. The huge NSA operations building is surrounded by a double chain-link fence with an enclosed minefield. As I remember, about 4,000 employees were housed in that one giant building. NSA spends its time listening to what the rest of the world is saying on radios, data links, telephones, and every other conceivable electronic link. It also breaks codes. Very spooky stuff.

NFOIO was the navy's only "all-source" intelligence analysis arm. We relied heavily on NSA's intercepts and augmented that information with everything else we could get our hands on to produce all-source intelligence for the navy's operational forces. Everything else included reports from legal travelers (business men, merchant sailors, and the like), ground photography, aircraft photography, and the take from our then very secret satellites.

Intelligence products were compartmented according to the collection source, and the compartments were assigned "codewords." For example, intelligence derived from communications intercepts (COMINT) might be classified TOP SECRET BEARTOOTH, or some such. Access to the information was limited on a strict need-to-know basis to protect the source, since, if the enemy knew we were listening in on a particular radio frequency, he could deny us the information by simply changing the frequency of his broadcasts. Until I reported to NFOIO, I thought TOP SECRET was as high as it went. Now I was to learn TOP SECRET was where it started. The many compartments one collected to do his job, while necessary, could present problems.

Before talking to a new colleague, it was necessary to check with the security people to see if he was cleared (briefed into) HOUNDS BREATH, or whatever. One signed a separate oath for each compartment, and the security folks kept track, although they were not cleared to read any of the product—they did not have a "need-to-know."

Order-of-Battle

I reported to the XO, and he told me I would be a Soviet naval surface ship order-of-battle analyst for the first year, then fleet up to be the submarine OOB analyst for the second year. For that first year, I would work under instruction to the submarine OOB analyst. An OOB analyst counts ships. The Soviets took great pains not to let us know how many and what kind of ships they had.

After my initial briefing, we went out into the work space to meet my new boss. He was a navy lieutenant, two years my senior. He was also a submariner. His name was Doug Lowrance, only son of Vice Admiral Rebel Lowrance. Could have knocked me over with a feather.

The admiral had known all this all along and had never breathed a word.

Time to buckle down and learn to be an intell weenie.

We kept big, four-inch-thick notebooks with a page for every ship we knew about. Each page was a calendar. Every time the ship came up on the radio and we intercepted the signal we made a color-coded mark on the appropriate day. Whenever a ship was sighted, we made a mark and noted the location. Ditto if she was photographed. If she was mentioned in a rare Soviet newspaper article we gleaned all the info we could and wrote it down. Sometimes we knew the captain's name. Sometimes we got the ship's repair schedule. It was like a big jigsaw puzzle. Great fun.

We were also starting to fingerprint radars. Every radar has a unique signature. As our equipment improved, we were trying to associate specific radars with their parent ships. Radio intercepts were called COMINT for communications intelligence. Other electronic emissions such as radar were called ELINT for electronic intelligence. A primary collection program consisted of specially configured Air Force planes that flew in international waters off the Soviet coasts and scooped up signals. And we were just beginning to fly intelligence satellites. The satellite stuff was so secret only about twelve of the hundred or so analysts in the office had a need-to-know. When a satellite dump was received, we went to a special room to see the take, which also included U-2 photographs. We were not allowed even to make notes. It was all pretty exciting.

Bobby Joe

Okay. Enough serious stuff.

Our office was populated for the most part by a bunch of young, bright, energetic naval officers, sailors, and civilians. We worked hard and produced professional intelligence product, but we were, well . . . young. And all work and no play makes Jack a dull boy.

Among our number was a naval aviator name of Bobby Joe. I remember his last name, but will keep it to myself in case this ever falls into the wrong hands. Bobby Joe was from Oglethorp, Georgia. Had managed to run his airplane out of gas in the Philippines and make an emergency landing on a rebel-held air strip. They let him go, but kept the plane. I think he was at NFOIO for a rest tour. Of course, he fit right in with the submariners, Marines, aviators, and other ne'er do wells. And Bobby was a bachelor.

Every morning about nine o'clock a designated secretary would make the rounds and take orders for doughnuts, sweet rolls, etc. to make a run to the cafeteria. Yes, in the mid-1960s, secretaries were still expected to make coffee and run errands.

Attractive young secretary comes up to Bobby's desk and asks if he wants anything from the cafeteria. Pencil poised. Bobby swivels his chair around and says in his thick Georgia accent: "Set on my lap while I decide."

She does.

We were young, remember? And sexual harassment hadn't been invented yet.

Bobby: "Get up! Get up!"

She does. Alarmed.

"What's wrong, Bobby Joe?"

Looking down at his lap, mournfully: "My momma told me if I ever let a purty girl set on my lap, I'd turn to stone. And it's already started!"

Oglethorp

We always thought the CIA guys were a little condescending. Snooty. Princeton.

We are at a conference at Langley (that's where the CIA lives). In uniform, for some reason. We normally worked in civvies. Sitting in the front row of the amphitheater. Couple of boring briefers in a row. Bobby Joe takes off his shoes and socks and begins to *clip his toe nails.* Jesus! CIA snobs are all staring at him . . . us. Only guys in the room in uniform. Representing the United States Navy, by god. Next briefer steps up and, looking directly at us, asks if everyone is cleared for DOG POO. We nod yes. Bobby continues to prune the toes, finishes while the briefer stumbles all over his presentation, and puts his shoes and socks back on. Gotta get ready. He's the next briefer.

Up to the podium. Confident. Looks smart in his uniform. Shined shoes. Newly pruned toes. Looks out at the CIA snobs and asks, "Is everyone cleared for OGLETHORP?" CIA guys all look at each other. Shoulder shrugs. Raised eyebrows. Negative head shakes. Bobby says, "OK. No problem. I'll leave that part out of my briefing." The son-of-a-bitch had just *invented a clearance out of thin air!*

Couple of days later, back at the ranch. The security guys descend on Bobby Joe like ugly on an ape. Mad as hell. Seems the CIA has filed a formal complaint the Navy is running a covert program, OGLETHORP, without their knowledge. The gumshoes are too dumb to even know where Oglethorp, Georgia, is.

Bobby got the last laugh. He made up a folder with all kinds of charts and graphs, stamped each page *TOP SECRET OGLETHORP EYES ONLY* and kept it in his desk to terrorize visitors.

The Jacket

A new submariner was reporting aboard. LCDR Jean Sheets, a well-known, well-liked colleague. He would run the current intelligence desk, providing the most up to date info on the Soviet fleet at sea to our guys at sea. Probably the most rewarding job in the office. Direct support to the troops on the front lines. Handpicked for the job.

As I said earlier, we normally worked in civilian clothes. None of us had much money, so some of the clothes were a bit well-worn. Somebody had donated a sports coat which was beyond repair. We had removed the sleeves and breast pocket and reinstalled them with fragile tack stitching. Waiting for a victim.

Jean reports for duty. XO welcomes him aboard. Escorts him out into the pits to see his desk and meet some folks. Doug Lowrance and I, being submariners, form a welcoming committee. Handshakes all around. Bobby Joe approaches, wearing the jacket. Tells Doug to "leave my woman alone."

Doug: "I'm busy here."

Bobby Joe: "I'm gonna have your ass."

Bobby shoves Doug.

Doug shoves Bobby Joe.

Back and forth.

Jean is wild-eyed.

Doug rips the pocket off the coat.

Bobby shoves again.

Doug rips a sleeve out.

Bobby says something incoherent.

Jean is looking for a foxhole to hide in.

Doug rips the other sleeve out.

XO has no idea what's going on.

Bobby Joe kisses Doug square on the lips,

Turns to Jean,

Sticks out his hand, and says:

"Welcome aboard."

Like I said, we were young.

The Admiral Visits

Our XO was a sweetheart. Good guy, good leader. He was also a line officer, eligible for command at sea. Our CO was, well, a puss. He was a staff officer, an intell weenie, not eligible for command at sea. Loyalty up, but none down. No big problem as the XO usually protected us. One morning the CO arrives at our work space in a tizzy-fit. Doug and I were reading the *Washington Post*, a great source for communist propaganda. Part of our jobs, right? Feet up on desks. Coffee at hand. The CO was *agitated. Big time.* He had a *vice admiral* in tow. A vice admiral, who happened to be in command of all the U.S. submarines in the Atlantic Fleet. **COMSUBLANT!** No other than Vice Admiral Vernon

L. Lowrance, USN. Himself! He had told the CO he wanted to meet the Soviet naval analysts.

Doug looks up, languidly.

"Hi, Dad."

I stand up. No blood kin here.

The admiral sticks out his hand and says, "Hi, Bruce."

The CO is about to swallow his tongue.

He knew about Doug, of course, but me?

Admiral says to me, "Remember when you screwed up my uniform medals? Payback time. Now you have to work for Doug."

A Place Called Vietnam

Watching warships was fun. Watching merchant ships was the pits. But it had to be done. We had a section that tracked communist merchants all over the world. Tried to find out their cargoes. Looked for them to deviate from their announced ports of call. It was all very important, but dull. The hottest analysts avoided the merchant desk.

One day the XO came wandering through the work spaces, looking for a volunteer to cover a place called Vietnam. Seems the brass downtown wanted more intelligence. Nobody was interested. Rinky-dink navy with a couple of old, worn-out coastal patrol boats. One of the junior civilian analysts, stuck in the merchant ship quagmire, saw a chance to escape and volunteered. We all thought he was mad.

When I retired in 1979, he was the senior civilian in the office of the Chief of Naval Intelligence. Some kinda foresight!

Back to Sea

After two years at NFOIO it was time to go back to sea. So far, I had been an Atlantic sailor. I wanted to see the Pacific and lobbied hard for a west coast boat. Finally orders arrived to USS *Razorback (SS 394)*, homeported in San Diego, California. I would be third officer. I was really excited. Much as I enjoyed NFOIO, I had joined the navy to see the world, and I was on my way.

But First the Mumps

Our house, awful as it was, sold quickly. Too quickly. We still had a couple of months before we detached, but the buyers wanted in now. We rented a furnished apartment in a less than attractive part of town.

It was tiny, but temporary. Then the boys came down with mumps. I had never had mumps. Contracting mumps at age twenty-nine is serious business for a male. Big problem! How do you isolate yourself when the entire living space for five people is about 600 square feet? Pat supervised. We managed. No mumps.

And We're Off

California, here we come. We had a Volkswagen bus. Took out the middle seat and sent it with the movers. Bought a 10 by 14 foot tent with all the trimmings and set out for San Diego via the Trans-Canada Highway, a trip of 5,000-plus miles. We never realized California is so long. Having had the same experience with Florida, we should have. But we didn't. The trip took thirty days and was a joy.

USS *Razorback (SS 394). Official U.S. Navy photo.*

Where to Start?

When we first saw the Pacific we all got out of the Volkswagen and waded into the surf. Everything on the west coast was backwards. When heading south, land was on the left, and the ocean was on the right. The current flowed south, not north (Japanese Current vs. Gulf Stream). The prevailing wind blew from the ocean, not from the

Appalachians. It was all very different and exciting.

Many naval officers had found a home in one ocean. There were Atlantic sailors and Pacific sailors. Nothing wrong with that, but I wanted to be a complete sailor and was overjoyed to be given the opportunity to serve in the world's biggest bathtub. As yet I had no concept of just how big the Pacific is.

We arrived in San Diego, checked into an efficiency motel, and I reported to the boat. Duty calls! It was a cheap motel in a Hispanic neighborhood. Never thought that I had the only set of wheels, we were in a strange town, none of our neighbors spoke English, she had three small babes to care for, and we had no permanent place to live. Off to work. We shortly found a house, rented it (from a tuna boat skipper), and got our furniture. I don't remember much about the motel. Was too excited about the new job.

Razorback

Razorback was a GUPPY submarine. *Irex* was a fleet snorkel with greater surface capabilities, but decreased submerged performance. *Razorback* had twice the batteries, lots of great electronic stuff, and was much quieter underwater. I had to qualify all over again. Luckily, like *Irex*, she was a Portsmouth boat (built in Portsmouth, New Hampshire, not at electric boat in New London), so the basic systems were familiar to me.

I was to be operations officer and navigator. Also, as third, I was senior watch officer. Big load? New ocean? No problem.

Shortly after I reported aboard, the boat departed for a four-month overhaul at Hunters' Point Shipyard in San Francisco. Quarters were available in the shipyard, but we elected for Pat and the kids to stay in San Diego so as not to disrupt the school year. I would live in the BOQ and commute on weekends when I could. As it worked out, I wound up working straight through on one weekend, then trading off duty assignments and taking a three-day break the next.

The Engineer is Top Gun in an overhaul. As Ops/Nav, I had to worry about the electronics stuff, but the workload was pretty light. As a result, and because I was fairly high in the pecking order and had some muscle, the skipper assigned me a bunch of odds and ends he wanted to get done.

Raising Your Hull Number

Our skipper was, to put it bluntly, a brown-nosing prick. He would do most anything to cultivate favor with his bosses. Comes the annual United Way campaign.

The catch-phrase of the year was "Raise Your Hull Number." The amount of $394 would have been no problem. But there was a catch. Add a zero. $3,940? With 100 men in the crew? No way. Skipper says, "Bruce, make it happen."

The officers slept in the BOQ. The troops slept on a barge which was moored to the pier. Bunkroom topside, office space below. On the main deck, we had installed Coke and candy machines. They were for the convenience of the crew, but also were used heavily by the civilian shipyard workers. A whole new source of funds, shipyard workers.

I went down to the red-light area of San Francisco and found a willing employee. She was a professional and we struck a legitimate, informal, but binding, commercial contract. Then on to promotion and advertising of *the raffle!*

I made a big sign to place next to the Coke machine.

Raffle!

Only $1.00

Winner gets to screw a whore in the bunkroom.

All other ticket holders get to take pictures.

Everybody a WINNER!

Tickets available from any Razorback crew member.

The shipyard workers—and sailors—ate it up. We already had sold a couple hundred dollars worth of tickets before the Old Man saw the sign. He went ballistic. Made me give the money back. Disappointed the whore—and the crew—and the shipyard workers. Made me go back on a valid contract. Bad image for the navy.

Redecorating

The CO's wife decided to redecorate the wardroom. Granted, the decor was masculine, but we were all guys. She could hold her own in a barracks knife fight, but her tastes ran to the feminine. Down came the tan curtains, replaced by a floral pattern. Out went the tan paint, replaced by a pinkish beige. And a floral centerpiece appeared in the center of the dinner table. Plastic flowers. The table was tiny. Barely enough room for plates and serving dishes, much less a bunch of fake flowers.

Late at night, as we sat playing cribbage, someone would light a cigarette and then use the old Zippo on the flowers. They melted in a most satisfying way. Lots of acrid smoke. After a while, the arrangement looked like London after the Blitz. El Capitano knew what was going on, of course, but to complain would have been to emulate the strawberry incident in *The Caine Mutiny*.

The XO

Our XO was a bachelor, a rarity in our mostly married wardrooms. He was a great, happy-go-lucky guy. Handsome. Smart dresser. Well spoken. Drove a Mercury Cougar, a muscle car. Just wasn't ready to settle down. The ladies loved him. He loved them, too. He was flirtatious, and they ate it up.

We are at a cocktail party one night. Miniskirts and low-cut tops are in. Pat is exposed top and bottom. John, our XO, admiring, reaches into his dead drink, retrieves a sliver of ice, and chucks it down the cleavage. Pat, looking him adoringly in the eye, grabs his belt, pulls, and pours *her* drink down the front of his trousers. Tough broad! Take a cold shower, Bud.

John received orders to command a submarine homeported in the Philippines. Made arrangements to ship the Cougar. Night before he left, we went into town and visited the Playboy Club. Very risqué in those days. He ordered a telephone brought to the table. Called a girl in Nebraska or somewhere and *proposed marriage!* Hearing the background noise, the lady asked him where he was. Playboy Club in San Francisco. She hung up. He couldn't figure out why.

Back to the BOQ. Very drunk. John pulls into the parking lot, right over one of those concrete markers meant to delineate the front of a parking space. Oops.

Next morning, a knock on my door. Hangover. Awful head. There's John in a dress uniform. "Come out to the parking lot."

There was the Cougar with a large pool of oil under her hood. Had torn out the oil pan. No problem. John signs a blank check, gives it to me, and tells me to get the car fixed. Use it until the overhaul is over, then ship it to him in the PI. I was sorry about the drip pan, but now I had wheels for the duration.

Conjugal Visit

Living in the BOQ allowed me to meet a number of naval reserve officers when they came in for their drill nights. They were local San Franciscans and knew all the small, good restaurants off the tourist path. I tried many of them and found some real favorites. Towards the end of the overhaul, I took a week's leave, got a room at the Marines' Memorial Hotel, and sent for the better half.

At the time, our black brethren were busy burning and looting the Bayview Community Center just outside the shipyard gates. These riots would become known as the Hunters' Point riots of 1966. They also were amusing themselves by shooting at municipal buses as they passed by. Riots notwithstanding, we sent a navy car to pick Pat up at the airport and deliver her to the shipyard.

We thoroughly enjoyed our little vacation and had a ball exploring the little bars and restaurants. One afternoon we needed to buy me a necktie. Going to a fancy place for dinner, and I didn't have one. We walked and shopped. Bought her some flowers from a street vendor. Bought a tie, fashionable at the time, wide enough to make her a bikini. Fond memories almost forty years later.

She left a pair of panties hanging on the gearshift of the Cougar just to make John envious.

The Pee Tube

When cruising on the surface, the lower reaches of the sail served as a men's room. When one felt the need, he would obtain permission from the OOD, drop down two decks from the bridge, and piss on the tank tops. Except in extremely calm weather, water washing over the tanks would flush the john, so to speak. In abnormally calm seas, the residue could get a little ripe.

Enter the engineer, a fastidious gent. While in the yard, he had installed a long pipe with a funnel affixed to the top. It started at the appropriate height on the bridge and descended to the waterline. He was very proud.

We got underway for sea trials. Captain on the bridge. Engineer comes up and points out his contribution to sanitation. Asks permission to demonstrate his relief system to the Old Man. Permission granted, he whips it out and begins. Trouble is, our erstwhile engineer had never been to college, nor exposed to Boyles' Laws of physics. The air flow over the funnel was creating a venturi effect, drawing air—and whatever else—*up the pipe.* Once he had a steady stream going, the urine came back up the tube, all over him, the lookouts, the OOD, and the CO. Best laid plans of mice and men . . .

The overhaul was over. Back to San Diego.

Big John and the Dachshund

The skipper was having a party. A costume party. A shipwreck costume party. Everyone was to dress accordingly. People came in all kinds of tattered clothes. Pat and I went black-tie formal. Figured the ship went down while we were dining.

The CO had a little dachshund of which he was inordinately fond. Dog was a crotch-sniffer and a leg-humper. Drove everybody crazy, especially the wives. CO thought it was cute. Enter Big John.

John was a former chief petty officer. He was at that time a LTJG. He was about six-four and all muscle. Had been in San Diego forever. He and Lorraine had been in the same quarters in navy housing for so long they had invested scarce funds and installed a chain-link fence around their yard. Had a whole passel of kids. Really great couple.

Having terrorized most of the women, the little wiener dog turned his attention to the men. Bad call. John was sitting on a couch when the dog sauntered up and began to hump his leg. John happened to be smoking a cigarette. He looked around to make sure the coast was clear, leaned over, lifted the dog's tail, and calmly stuffed the cigarette up its ass—business end first. Dog takes off like a rocket—howling. CO is on his knees trying to calm the animal. Baby-talking it. Disgusting. Big John lights another cigarette and goes to the kitchen for a fresh drink, wearing the biggest grin you ever saw.

Fang

The captain's family was rounded out by a five-year-old boy we called Fang. His front baby teeth had been knocked out in an auto accident, and his second teeth were still somewhere in the future.

We were scheduled for a dependents' cruise. These cruises were always a lot of fun. They provided an opportunity for the wives to see their guys at work and for the sailors to show off a bit. For safety reasons, kids had to be twelve or older to come along. Unless you were the captain. He made an exception for his son, thus pissing off all the other crewmen with small children. Furthermore, he and his wife wanted to play host and hostess, and the monster was in the way. No problem. Assign the third officer to babysit.

I was baby-sitting the kid in my stateroom, trying to keep him occupied. Reading blueprints to him or something. We were a little short on toys, and his folks had neglected to bring any along. Suddenly, without warning, the little bastard leans over and *bites my leg*. Hard! His snaggly fangs get entangled in my pants, and I can't shake him loose. So I get him by the ears and try to break his bulldog grip. He's screaming bloody murder when I hear a deep voice over my shoulder asking, "What are you doing to my son?" Oh, shit. It was Fang's mom.

Luckily, she didn't write my fitness reports. She never did believe I was the victim.

Plane Crash

There was a serious side to life. We were operating off San Clemente Island, giving ping time (serving as a target) to some destroyers and aircraft. Most of the ASW (antisubmarine warfare) aircraft were P3s, but in this case we were working with some smaller, rather old S2s. They had a crew of four. In the wee hours of the morning, we heard a loud explosion on sonar followed by classic breaking-up sounds. We surfaced immediately and tried to call our airdale buddy on the radio. No luck. They had augered in. The destroyers hadn't realized it yet. We started an immediate search. The destroyers used their big search-lights until they burned them out.

Suddenly we saw a dim strobe light. The kind that are attached to life jackets. There was a life raft! Our swimmer goes over the side. Grabs the life-raft. Two guys in it. One had both legs broken. The force of the impact had torn off both of his high-top lace-up boots. Got both men on deck. The guy with the broken legs was unconscious, but breathing. Our guys lowered him below so our corpsman could work on him. Second guy was terrified of going below. Claustrophobic. We finally got him off the main deck, down the ladder, and into the boat, but he was very uncomfortable. Said submarines were dangerous—and he had just ridden an airplane into the sea.

Next morning, we found only bits and pieces of floating debris, including the left half of the pilot's helmet. It was a sad experience and reminded us all of our vulnerability.

Puget Sound

Our next assignment was to go to Puget Sound to test some new gear and fire torpedoes on the calibrated range. We were also due to get a new skipper, and I was ready to be promoted to LCDR.

New Skipper

We were moored to a pier at the Puget Sound Naval Base. Pouring cats and dogs. Our new CO was due and excitement ran high. The skipper's navy car was all cleaned. The duty driver was in dress blues. We were expecting a call at any moment to come pick up the new boss.

Couple of shore patrol came aboard, dripping rain water and indignation. Wanted to know about a stolen forklift parked on the pier. We knew nothing. Very mysterious. Shore patrol left, mumbling to themselves.

Out of the shadows appeared the new CO. Soaking wet. Lugging his B-4 bag (sailors carry their gear in a sea bag, officers in a B-4 bag, a sort of canvas suitcase). Captain Billy had arrived. He hadn't been able to get a ride from the base duty officer, so he had *commandeered an unattended forklift and driven it a couple of miles to the boat!* In the pouring rain. We're gonna like this guy! Not like his predecessor, Charlie Tuna, Chicken of the Sea. This guy had a set of gonads.

Lieutenant Commander, United States Navy

The navy has a saying. "Young studs, old fuds, and lieutenant commanders." Young studs are junior officers in need of much supervision. Old fuds are senior officers in need of Viagra. Lieutenant commanders are squarely in between. I had been on the selection list for some time, and now my number was up. Pin on the gold oak leaves. I would now be recognized as a career naval officer, a lifer. As was the custom, I hosted a party at the club, and everyone drank to my promotion. Unbeknown to me, this was to be the first of three wetting down parties for my new half stripe.

Change of Command

Command in the military is everyone's goal. In the navy, command at sea is particularly meaningful. Remember the merchant navy term master? Master after God. Command entails a tremendous amount of responsibility. And reward. Change of command ceremonies reflect the importance of the institution.

The crew is paraded in dress uniform. The guests, in their finest attire, are seated formally on chairs dressed up with starched cotton covers. The outgoing skipper makes a speech and reads his orders. The new skipper reads his (never gives a speech; he hasn't earned the right yet). The new guy salutes the old guy and says, "I relieve you, sir." The old guy returns the salute and says, "I stand relieved." The new commanding officer turns to his immediate superior, salutes, and reports, "I have assumed command of USS *Razorback,* sir." The superior returns the salute and acknowledges, "Very well." The ritual is all very formal and dates back hundreds of years. Lord Nelson's ceremonies probably were identical.

We are back in San Diego. Ready for the change of command. Wind is whipping. Mooring lines are groaning under the strain. Ladies are holding on to their hats. Officers have tied down theirs with the chin straps. Ceremony is over. Everybody proceeding to the Officers' Club for the reception. Big John Cameron is the OOD.

Party trailing down the pier. Big John appears on deck. Yells, "Charlie!" to the outgoing skipper. Unheard of. He still rates being called captain. Remember the plastic wardroom flowers? The ones we melted? John has the wardroom flower arrangement in hand. Eyes gleaming. "You forgot your flowers." *Heaves them over the side!* Oh, my.

Wetting Down II

The first time I went to the O Club wearing my new stripe, it was drinks all around. This was, of course, for my friends who had not been in Puget Sound for Wetting Down I.

Wetting Down III

My new stripe was getting a bit soggy, but the wardroom wives had not yet been included, so off we went for WD-III. The party was to be at our house, and the main attraction a concoction called Fish House Punch. You were supposed to mix a bunch of liquor and add ginger ale to dilute the brew. I decided to substitute champagne for ginger ale. Mistake #1.

It was fashionable at the time to freeze fruit and add it to the punch bowl as a combination cooler and decoration. Pat froze up a bunch of strawberries and such in their own juice. Big blocks. Very pretty. As they floated and melted, the fruits themselves drifted free from the block of ice. Flotsam, as it were. Many of the guests spooned a berry or two into their cups. Very festive. Unbeknown to us, the berries absorbed alcohol at a great rate. Mistake #2.

Our new XO was a near teetotaler. He nursed a cup of punch early on, but then switched to plain fruit as the melting progressed. Multiple cups. No harm, right? Fruit is good for you. An apple a day and so forth. Not Fish House Punch alcoholic fruit! Mistake #3.

Long before the shank of the evening, XO was taking a nap on the couch. Flat on his back. Snoring peacefully. We crossed his arms on his breast, put a flower in his hands, and took photographs for posterity . . . and blackmail. What a party.

More on the New XO

I'd had good XOs and bad ones. This one was a little bit of an old lady, but undoubtedly the hardest working, most conscientious with whom I had been privileged to sail. Only a year senior to me, he took my harassment with grace and dignity. His first thought was always for the troops.

He was a devout Catholic. Unfortunately, he and his wife had been unable to conceive, but had adopted two lovely children. Our extended periods at sea had been hard on the wife, and she had been receiving counseling from their priest and seemed to be making progress.

We lived a few blocks up the street from them. One evening, after we had just returned from a couple of weeks at sea, there was a knock at our door. There stood the XO.

When he had arrived home, his wife told him the priest was coming by. The priest appeared in due course, not to continue the counseling, but to announce that he and the wife were in love and planned to marry. What a blow to this most devout man! Deceived by a priest.

The priest resigned. The wife got an annulment— no natural children. And they were married. Hopefully, to rot in hell.

Off to WESTPAC

After a shipyard overhaul and a retraining/workup period, boats routinely made a six-month deployment to the Western Pacific (WESTPAC). Although dreading the family separation, we were excited about getting back to sea. After all, most of us had joined the navy to see the world. I was about to find out just how big the Pacific Ocean is.

Setting the Clocks

The world is divided into time zones. As one sails west, the clocks are set back every fifteen degrees of longitude. This makes the sun rise and set at a reasonable hour. Local time is calculated for the entire zone based on the center of the zone. The whole system starts in England with Greenwich Mean Time (GMT). San Diego is on plus seven, or seven hours earlier than GMT. Hawaii is on plus fifteen.

Normally, when making a transit, a ship sets the clock ahead or back one hour at a time, much like we do with Daylight Savings Time. Since watches at sea are stood on a four-hour basis around the clock, actual local time makes little difference. One can eat breakfast in the middle of the night or supper at sunrise with little or no inconvenience. On the other hand, changing the clock one hour at a time causes some five-hour watches. I decided to set the ship's clocks to Pearl Harbor time in one fell swoop on leaving San Diego to avoid the elongated watches. Didn't bother the crew one bit. Damned near killed me. I was getting up in the middle of the night to shoot stars, going to bed in the middle of the day, and so on. Never got into a routine. Live and learn.

Overcast

In those days, we navigated by the stars and sun. No satellite geopositioning. As sailors had done since time began, I shot morning and evening stars and local apparent noon (LAN) when the sun was directly overhead. The chief quartermaster and I would each take a sextant to the bridge and shoot five stars. Then we would lay below and plot them. We would compete for the tightest fix. A good fix was accurate to about a half mile. We then would project our position ahead by dead reckoning (DR) based on our course and speed and the prevailing ocean currents and winds. Subsequent star fixes were used as corrections. All well and good if one can see the stars.

At certain times of the year, great portions of the Pacific are covered with a high, thin cloud layer. Stars are invisible. The sun shines through, but LAN produces only a latitude (north/south) position. We left the San Diego sea buoy in good shape. Got good radar cuts on San Clemente Island. Got maybe one good star fix after that. Then nothing. For days on end. No stars.

Our course and speed readings were accurate, and we had charts predicting ocean currents. But those were merely predictions, and winds acting on our big sail were another factor. The combination of wind and currents could drift us far off our intended course.

As required by navy regulations, I reported to the captain three times a day giving him our position, but after a few days, it was nothing more than an educated guess. He was very patient. I began to realize how big the ocean is and how small the Hawaiian Islands. Look at a map some day. Those tiny specks out there are the only dry land for miles and miles.

Our surface radar could pick up land at about thirty miles. I had visions of missing Hawaii altogether. But we also had a crude radio direction finder (RDF) capability. We normally used it to get a bearing on a ship or aircraft radar. It was accurate to no more than about five degrees. But its range could be as great as a hundred miles. Much farther than the radar. Idea! Hawaii had a number of commercial radio stations. We already had tuned in to one for the crew's entertainment.

We looked up all the stations on Hawaii, got their frequencies, and started an RDF search. Inaccurate as the bearings were, they were better than nothing. After a few hours of hard plotting, the chief and I concluded we were about fifty miles from where we thought we were. Reported same to the captain and asked to alter course seventy degrees. That's a *big* turn. He was unruffled . . . said go ahead. A few hours later we picked up land on the radar. We had found Hawaii! I felt like Captain Cook.

Paymaster

After a brief stay at Pearl Harbor, we set off for Yokosuka, Japan. On arrival, the XO told me to get hold of the shipyard people and arrange for the troops to be paid. We carried the pay records on board for just that reason. I merely had to call the base supply folks, deliver the records to them, and arrange for them to come on board and pay the crew. Simple.

I got a female chief petty officer on the phone. Whiskey voice. In those days, there were few female sailors, much less chief petty officers.

"Chief, this is LCDR Schick on the submarine *Razorback*. I need to get the crew paid."

"Yeah, and this is Abraham Lincoln."

Hung up.

I call back. Same message.

Chief says, "Look, wiseass. I'm busy."

Hung up again.

I got the records and humped up to the supply office. Found the chief. She was sporting a three-day beard. Tough as nails. Introduced myself. She put down her cigar.

"I apologize, Mr. Schick. But I'm very busy and don't need crank phone calls. The guy who put LCDR Schick on the *Razorback* had a real sense of humor."

I had never made the connection between Schick, a major manufacturer of razor blades, and *Razorback.* She promptly renamed me LCDR *Gillette* for the remainder of our stay. We became great drinking buddies. By the way, she was the only female allowed in the stag bar at the Chiefs' Club.

SpecOps

Soon enough we were off on a special operation (SpecOp). These operations were, and are, highly classified. For an excellent, detailed account, read *Blind Man's Bluff,* by Sherry Sontag and Christopher Drew. Suffice it to say that SpecOps were intelligence gathering missions. Much has been written of them in the open literature. I am still bound by an oath of silence, so I won't tell you where we went. I will tell you we stayed in international waters (more than three miles offshore) and did nothing illegal. On the other hand, we were in harm's way and conducting real world operations, not exercises. SpecOps were the *raison d'être* for submariners.

The idea was to loiter offshore and collect information on the enemy navy. We listened to radio transmissions, radars, and underwater communications. We took photos. We had a ball.

Our assigned area consisted of very shallow water for hundreds of miles. Shallow to a submariner is anything less than two hundred feet. Six hundred is what we crave. Deeper water allows a boat to go deep and get under the keel of passing ships. This is a convenient way to avoid collisions.

Junks

Our area had lots of merchant traffic. It was easy to predict where a merchant ship was going and get out of her way. There were also a lot of oceangoing junks. Most of them were sail-powered. Because junks are flat-bottomed with no keel, they tend to crab with the wind. That is, they don't sail straight ahead, but slightly sideways.

The captain had standing orders that we were to call him whenever a contact looked like it was going to come within four thousand yards (two nautical miles). We were to avoid getting that close if we could. Because he was also a heavy sleeper, we knew if we woke him at night, he'd need a shot of caffeine. He drank his coffee "blond and sweet," with a large dollop of sugar and a shot of powdered cream.

Picture this. Middle of the night. Dark as the inside of a hat. Here comes a damn junk. We're snorkeling, recharging batteries. Maneuver to avoid. No luck. Junk is skating sideways.

Call the wardroom. "Blond and sweet to the conning tower."

Call the skipper. "Got a junk up here. Gonna pass close aboard."

"Very well, be right up."

Himself arrives. Hand him the coffee.

He sits on the bench and sips.

I'm locked onto the periscope. Using speed to avoid.

Wasting precious amps.

Himself lights a cigarette. "How we doing?'

"OK, Skipper. I think he'll pass clear."

The junk passes so close aboard I can see a guy sitting on deck smoking a cigarette. Can see the glow of the butt when he takes a drag. *Jesus!*

"OK, Skipper, we're clear."

"Good job. Call me if you need help again."

Back to bed. Damn, it was fun!

"Snorkel Deep Into . . ."

We operated in daylight hours on the battery. Quiet. Antennas and periscope up. Snooping. The nucs can do this forever. But, alas, we had to recharge the battery every day. This required snorkeling. When we snorkeled, we put up an air intake as big as a garbage can, started two engines, and charged batteries. Noisy.

To increase our chances of remaining undetected, we would relocate offshore a little farther before lighting off the engines. To simplify things and to ensure we followed a random pattern, we laid out ten mile squares on the chart for night operating areas. We inked them in on the chart and then laminated it with a new stuff called Mylar. It was great—came in three foot rolls, sticky on one side. Laminate the chart and you could write on it each night, then erase it for the next night.

Every captain establishes his own standing night orders. They instruct the OOD as to the basic wishes of the skipper. Some COs are very cautious, some give more leeway to the OOD. Augmenting the standing orders is the night order book. It provides specific, often time-sensitive direction. For example, it might direct: "Call me when you sight the New London Ledge lighthouse." Normally, the engineer makes the first entries, specifying what he needs done. Then the Ops officer would add his guidance. Then the CO would review their orders, add his own, and sign the page. At that point, the night orders became an official, direct command from the captain. Before posting the watch, the oncoming OOD would read and initial the night orders. In our case the night orders would direct the OOD to proceed to a designated snorkel area and charge batteries for the next day.

As navigator, I got to lay out the night snorkel areas. As I said before, ten-mile squares. To facilitate writing the night orders, we named each one after the officers' wives. Thence:

"At 1630, depart patrol area and proceed to Area Cindy.

On arrival, snorkel deep into Cindy for the remainder of the night.

Be alert for naval contacts.

Depart Cindy at 0430 to arrive on station by first light."

CO and CO_2

We would spend sixteen hours or more a day submerged at periscope depth on the batteries with no outside ventilation. During that time everyone was breathing. We humans breath in oxygen and exhale mostly carbon dioxide (CO_2). The cooks were cooking meals, burning oxygen (O_2) and emitting god knows what. Most of us smoked cigarettes, burning O_2 and emitting CO_2 and carbon monoxide (CO). Enough chemistry?

By the end of each day, we all had splitting headaches. Breathing was difficult. Zippo lighters would not ignite—too little O_2. We found that matches would, so we could continue to smoke cigarettes. Then came the long-awaited order: "Prepare to snorkel. Two engines."

VROOOOOOM. Engines light off. Sucking air into the boat. Air. Blessed, fresh, pure air. Coursing through the boat. Manually shut the snorkel intake valve. Pull a two-inch vacuum. Engines sucking more air. Burning the CO and the CO_2. Purge the boat! God, it felt good.

If you've never had this experience, you cannot really appreciate a crisp autumn day.

Craps

Gambling on a naval vessel is illegal. The troops played poker and pinochle for small change and the officers overlooked it. The chief of the boat was under strict orders to police the card games and make sure no one got in over his head. The system worked well.

The officers mostly played bridge, acey-deucey, and cribbage. I don't remember ever playing for money. We were expected to set an example. But the new skipper was a crapshooter par excellence. Loved to roll those bones. Mostly with chief petty officers.

The chiefs' bunk room was called the "goat locker." It measured about 6 by 12 feet and housed up to eleven bodies. Pretty crowded. Had a curtain that pulled over the door for privacy.

Late into the wee hours of the morning, you could hear the skipper, down on his knees in the goat locker behind that thin curtain imploring those bones. "Seven, come eleven." The crew loved it.

Selling Spares: Serious Stuff

We made a port call in Kao-hsiung on the northern edge of Taiwan. Great liberty. Because of the ongoing trouble between Taiwan and mainland China, there was a strict curfew on the piers and in the waterfront area. Armed soldiers patrolled at night. One night all hell broke loose on the pier. Gunshots, whistles, shouting. The OOD rushed topside only to find a couple of the crew being held on the pier at gunpoint by a bunch of Taiwanese soldiers. Our guys were carrying gunny sacks full of spare parts they were going to sell on the black market.

Even our easygoing, crapshooting captain had to crack down hard. Courts-martial are never pleasant, but he busted the culprits one stripe, with another suspended. That meant if they misbehaved again, the CO could vacate the suspension and take another stripe. Losing two pay grades is a big deal. It wipes out about six years of hard work. The troops got the message.

On to Chi-lung

After operating with the Taiwanese navy for a while, we proceeded to Chi-lung on the south coast. Located there was a true gem of the Orient: Alice's Palace.

Alice's Palace was a five- or six-story hotel. On the ground floor were shops with oriental crafts and souvenirs. They were of surprisingly good quality and well priced. On the second floor was a first-class saloon. The drinks were inexpensive and not watered. On the third floor was a wonderful restaurant. Gourmet Chinese food. And yes, the meals were great and cheap. The fourth floor offered clean, inexpensive rooms to sailors. And the fifth and sixth were a whorehouse.

Alice was a tiny Chinese woman well past her working days. She was married to a retired American chief petty officer who had "gone Asiatic." When he retired from the navy, he stayed in Taiwan, married Alice, and opened an "honest whorehouse/restaurant." He looked after the troops like a father. If they got too drunk, he installed them in a room. Made sure he had their valuables for safekeeping. The girls were medically inspected and certified. He held reveille in the morning and piled all the troops into taxicabs to get them back to the ship on time. He said he had been rolled in too many dives in his time and wanted to provide a safe harbor for sailors of the world. Sort of like a seagoing Wal-Mart. Labor of love (pardon the pun). What a guy!

The Scotch Vapors

Time to head for San Diego. We pointed the bow east and poured on the coal. Put into Guam to refuel and take on fresh stores. There was a message from the previous CO asking us to pick up a case of Cutty Sark for him. Duty free. Dollar a bottle. And then smuggle it past Customs.

We bought the case. Brought it on board. First night out the skipper wondered if that Scotch was potable. We cracked a bottle to check. Next night we tested another. Then a third, and so forth. We carefully resealed all the bottles full of fumes, and put them back in their cardboard box. Told the old CO the whiskey must have evaporated when we snorkeled.

A Second Pacific Boat

I had been in *Razorback* for two years and was due to rotate out. Called BuPers and they said I would be ordered to USS *Volador (SS 490)* as XO. The good news was she was a San Diego boat. The bad news, she was getting ready to deploy to WESTPAC.

USS *Volador (SS490). Official U.S. Navy photo.*

Volador, like *Razorback*, was a GUPPY III conversion of a WWII submarine. She was also a Portsmouth boat so once again I was familiar with the engineering systems. When we got back from WESTPAC, I took a family break, got a fresh haircut, and shined my shoes. I would be relieving a classmate from Annapolis. I didn't know the skipper.

First Impressions

With my new haircut and spit-shined shoes, I decided to pay a call on my new home. The topside watch saluted and answered my "request permission to come aboard" in a proper fashion. He volunteered to summon the duty officer. I replied I'd find my own way.

I walked aft and slid down the After Battery hatch, which lead directly into the crew's mess. Couple of sailors were sitting at a table playing cards. One whispered, "Who the hell is that?" Other said, "I don't know. But look at the haircut on that bastard." My hair was *short*. Point made. Rule: You can start off tough and back off over time. You can't start out easy and then try to tighten up. Final comment from the troops: "Jesus Christ. That's the new XO!" So much for first impressions.

The Walk-through

A turnover is about what you would imagine. Go over the ship's administrative records, personnel files, training records, other paperwork and pass on any additional relevant information. The final step is a walk through the boat, the incomer asking the outgoer whatever questions come to mind. Keep in mind the XO is responsible to the CO for the overall condition of the boat. *Volador* was *filthy*. Dirt and grime everywhere. Faded, peeling paint. Soiled decks. Even the galley, normally immaculate, was a mess. My predecessor seemed to think this all was normal. I held my tongue and relieved him. Then we symbolically reported to the captain. "I have relieved Mr. X as executive officer of *Volador*, Captain."

"Very well. What did you think of the boat?"

"She's filthy, Captain, but I'll get her squared away."

How dumb can you get? First time out of the blocks with a new skipper and I tell him his boat is filthy. He never really forgave me— but I got the boat cleaned up.

The Phantom Move

We had moved from our original rental house in the Portuguese fishermen's quarter of San Diego to another on Point Loma, all the while waiting for navy housing. I had been near the top of the waiting list as a lieutenant (junior housing), then made lieutenant commander and went to the bottom of the senior officer waiting list. This didn't seem fair, and I asked the squadron to intervene. There was some urgency in view of our imminent departure for WESTPAC. We were deep into our predeployment workup and training.

We arrived back in port early one week, and Pat and the boys were not on the pier to meet me. I figured one of the guys was sick and bummed a ride home. All the lights were off. I peered in the windows and saw nothing. Pounded on the door. Rang the bell. Nothing. Worry set in fast. Had there been an auto accident? Had a parent back east died, and Pat and the kids flown back? Had they been kidnapped by the drugged-out hippies who ruled San Diego in the late '60s?

I went next door to our kindly, elderly neighbors. Pat loved him because he took nude sunbaths in their yard. Always waved to her as he strolled in the all-together from the house to his chaise lounge.

Navy housing had become available, and Pat had moved. No, they didn't know the address. And no, the phone company had not yet hooked up a telephone. Our neighbors piled me in their car and we took a tour of navy housing, looking for our venerable Blue Bus. And there it was. Parked outside a house whose front yard was littered with empty packing boxes. Home at last. The boys were playing castles in some cut-up boxes. As I walked up the sidewalk, one looked up, said casually, "Hi, Dad," and went back to playing. So much for worrying.

A Very Brief Visit

After what seemed only a few days, we were headed back to WESTPAC. Now, on my second trip, I was an old hand. Had "recent experience" according to the staff. A veritable font of knowledge.

And an Awful Departure

When a boat deployed on a long trip, the pier was crowded with wives and kids in their finest, staff officers looking envious, and a navy band. Some of the wives cried. Most kept a stiff upper lip until we were underway. The kids looked bewildered. The staff assured us they would look after our families. The band played martial music.

We set the maneuvering watch and started the engines. Snubbed the bow in tight to the pier so the screws were clear. Took in all but number one mooring line. XO reports, "The ship is ready to get underway, Captain."

"Very, well. Officer of the Deck, get underway."

OOD: "Take in number one. All back two thirds."

Billowing diesel smoke. Churning white water aft. Many wives crying now.

The Old Man takes off his wedding band and puts it in his pocket. Then holds up a cassette player and plays the popular country song *"Please release me, let me go"* at top volume. Whatever wives were not crying before were now. Many from sheer rage. What an ass.

P. C. Stryker

Our Ops/Nav was a former enlisted man named Phil Stryker. He had been a chief electrician, then got commissioned as a Limited Duty Officer (LDO). This commission would have confined him to engineering duties. Not good enough for Stryker! All or nothing. Against all advice, he converted to line officer (eligible for command at sea). This meant he would have to compete with college grads. He heartily despised, not necessarily college grads, but those who had come up the easy way instead of the hard way through the ranks. He was especially unfond of ring knockers (Naval Academy alumni). He was seven years older than I, had ten years more in the navy, and had been in the Pacific since Noah ordered him there. But I was senior.

Phil was a gadget guy. Loved the new electronic navigation stuff that was just being introduced to the fleet. Nothing wrong with that. But you will remember I felt strongly about the tradition of celestial navigation. Besides, what if all those fancy satellites crashed? Suffice it to say, I forced him to shoot stars. Pissed him off, too.

According to his wife, Francine, we were two hardheaded Prussian bastards, but we were professionals. Phil would come knock on my door. "XO, I need permission to do so and so."

"Nah, Phil. I think you should do such and such."

"Goddamn it, Bruce, you are the dumbest asshole I ever met."

"Tough shit, Stryker. Make it happen."

"OK, but it's your fault when it fucks up. Wanna go to the club for lunch and a beer?"

Drove the rest of the wardroom and the crew crazy. They couldn't figure how we could compartmentalize our lives so well.

Acey-Deucey

Boredom is perhaps your greatest enemy at sea. Rent a DVD of *Das Boot,* preferably the director's uncut version, and you will understand what I mean. Submarine sailors played cards, grew beards, read books, lifted weights, sharpened knives until they were like razors, told lies, and slept a lot. Strykee and I played a lot of cribbage. It's a rather simple game. Fast moving. One counts points as the cards are played and again at the conclusion of each hand. Simple. But we would *cheat.* Not casually. *The object was to cheat.* If you cheated and won, you were honor bound to point out your transgressions to you opponent, cackling gleefully, as in, "I clipped you for three points on that last hand, you dumb-shit." Likewise, if you caught your adversary in the act, you pleaded shocked outrage. "You cheating son of a bitch. I'll never play with you again."

We were easily amused. After a while, we played with two, then three combined decks. Got to where nobody could figure the odds, much less keep score. By the way, we kept a running score for an entire seven-month deployment. Cheated on that, too.

Phil's dead now. Died of cancer. I wonder if he's found a cribbage partner in heaven? Or is he waiting for me? Probably both . . . certainly he's practicing his cheating while he waits.

The Vertical Swimming Pool

On the way to WESTPAC, we stopped in Pearl Harbor. Got some briefings. Requalified in the escape tower. The escape tower is a swimming pool about twenty feet in diameter and 150 feet deep. It has pressure locks (rooms) at fifty-foot intervals. To requalify, one had to go down the outside to fifty feet, climb into the lock, and be pressurized to a level equal to fifty feet underwater. When the air pressure was equalized with that in the water, a hatch was opened, and you entered the tank and swam to the surface. This simulated escaping from a sunken submarine. It was scary, but not dangerous. It was, however, imperative that you kept blowing air out as you ascended. Air expands as the square of the pressure, and you were in danger of bursting a lung if you didn't exhale. The problem was, your lungs felt starved for air, and it was hard to keep blowing. Divers were stationed along the ascension and would pull you over into a little air lock if they didn't see bubbles. Our corpsman was in charge of the escape training.

The skipper needed a drinking buddy. By tradition, he couldn't fraternize with the crew, and he was reluctant to get too close to the wardroom. I was it. We'd been in port about two days, and I'd not drawn a sober breath. Time for us to go swimming.

We arrived at the tank in the bag. Got into our bathing suits. Our corpsman, one Doc Linahan, arrived to escort us to the pool. "Captain, have you all been drinking?" Silly question. We smelled like a barroom floor. Captain: "Just a few beers, Doc."

"I can't let you go through the tank, sir."

"I'm the captain, Doc. Lead on."

"I can't do that, Captain."

"Damn it, man. Do as I say."

"OK, sir. But if y'all drown, don't blame me."

We made it. Cakewalk. Doc never forgave us. I think he was secretly hoping we'd drown.

The *Pueblo* Bunch

Wherever possible, submariners create their own club rather than frequent the Main Base Officers' Club. At Pearl Harbor it was in the submarine BOQ. Handy to have the bar in the same building we were staying in. You could crawl from the bar to bed.

We were imbibing a few one evening when the door flew open and the *Pueblo* wardroom breezed in. Remember *Pueblo?* Her skipper was Pete Bucher, a submariner. Coincidentally, he was an old buddy of Phil Stryker's. The rate of alcohol consumption increased as we welcomed our new friends. We all went down to the pier and toured *Pueblo*. Back to the club.

The after-hours bar was upstairs. At the bottom of the stairwell were a couple of stainless steel carts on wheels. The stewards used them to carry dirty dishes. The wheels were little, like supermarket carts. But in our state of advanced inebriation, they were *Roman chariots!* Races! One guy lying on the cart, one pushing. Not up and down the halls. No. We were submariners! *Up and down the staircases.* Mostly down. Lots of crashes. Lots of noise. Lots of wrecked carts. Little did we know that in a matter of weeks, our *Pueblo* shipmates would be in North Korean prison camps after she was captured.

The Pearl City Tavern, or Monkey See, Monkey Do

Pearl City is a few miles north of Pearl Harbor. It is mostly a collection of substandard houses and sailor bars. Preeminent among the latter was the Pearl City Tavern. The PCT had a bar about fifty feet long. Behind the bar on the wall was a fifty-foot glass cage full of monkeys. The patrons sat at the bar and drank and stared at the monkeys. The monkeys did monkey things.

We were into Harvey Wallbangers, a potent drink consisting of orange juice and vodka topped with a floating shot of Gallianno. They go down *smooth*. We sat at the bar. Drinking Harvey Wallbangers. Watching the monkeys. Until we realized *the monkeys were watching us*. Sobering thought.

Off to Yokosuka

First stop in WESTPAC was the shipyard at Yokosuka in Tokyo Bay. It had been a major Japanese shipyard in WWII. MacArthur had spared it for our use after the war. It had not been bombed.

As in Pearl Harbor, there was a submarine BOQ and club. It was called the Submarine Sanctuary. There were bunkrooms, each assigned to a visiting submarine wardroom. There was another called XOs' Haven, where the XOs slept, and another called COs' Haven. There was a closed mess where we took our meals. Last but not least was a sitting room/lounge/bar equipped with pool tables, Ping-Pong tables, and a movie projector converted to run on fifty-cycle (Japanese) electricity. The bartender was a guy named Benny who had been skipper of a Japanese destroyer in WWII.

On the ship's initial visit of a deployment, every officer was charged $50. For the rest of the trip, this deposit covered your laundry, bedding, and towels at the sanctuary. Each time you arrived, there was a freshly starched *yokata* laid out on your bunk. A yokata is an informal kimono, used as a bathrobe. It really felt great to get off that smelly submarine, take a long hot shower, get into a fresh clean starched yokata, and down an icy beer.

Benny went off duty about ten o'clock each night. After that drinks were on the honor system. You mixed your own and put the money in a cigar box. The bar never closed.

There was a strict rule not to let Benny drink. But every once in a while the rule got bent. Then its purpose became obvious to all. Benny could not hold his booze. First he was a weepy drunk. No big problem. He would recall his glory days on his destroyer in WWII. Had some great sea stories to tell. Then he would remember his side lost. He'd get a little moribund. Then he'd remember who had won—us! Then he became a samurai warrior. The bastard kept a *sword* under the bar. Made believers of us all when he came up over the bar, brandishing the sword and shouting, *"Banzai."* Luckily, by that time, he was easily disarmed.

Korea

We were scheduled to provide services to the South Korean navy. We would submerge during the day and give them ping time. At night, they would assign us an area to steam on the surface while they went off to hunt for North Korean infiltrators. The two Koreas still considered themselves in a state of war. One night, a destroyer came up in a big hurry and told us to remain in the area and turn on our Grimes light, a large yellow rotating light like you see on tow trucks in the United States. Turns out they had sonar contact on an unidentified submarine.

They requested permission from the beach to drop depth charges, but were denied. Not to be overcome, they lowered their anchor to 200 feet and trolled all night. Those guys were tough.

After a couple weeks' operations, we made Pusan for a port call and some liberty. The Koreans threw a big bash for the troops and a fancy reception for the officers. They were very eager to impress us with their knowledge of American ways. Had an elaborate bar set up. American bar. Johnny Walker Black Label Scotch and tonic. Nothing but the best for their American friends. Ever drink a Scotch and tonic?

Siamese Sea

Next we serviced the Thai navy. The Gulf of Siam is shallow and subject to violent storms. Sure enough, a real humdinger blew up. The Thai admiral took his destroyers to a safe harbor and told us to find one of our choosing to wait out the storm. We did, in the leeward shadow of a tiny island. We anchored and could see a little thatch-roofed village with people walking along the beach. The storm passed on, and the wind subsided. Skipper called me topside. He was on the main deck, glassing the beach with his binoculars. "XO, prepare the landing party to go ashore. Break out the rubber boat."

We had one twelve-man rubber raft that had never been broken out except for inspections. Brought it topside. Got it out of its bag. Weighed a ton. Lots of talcum powder floating around. Inflated it. Veritable clouds of talc. Mustered the landing party. Sent them ashore with orders to rent a boat with a motor. The life raft had only oars.

Pretty soon a fishing boat puttered out from the village. We traded 100 pounds of coffee for shuttle services. Sent the liberty party ashore.

We were sending a military force onto a foreign island without permission from the navy, the State Department, or the Thai government. But who cared?

Turns out the village had a restaurant, a bar, and a whorehouse. Unfortunately, half the liberty party came down with clap. Sounded like a rain forest in the crew's quarters.

Bangkok for Christmas

Finished with providing services, we were ordered to Bangkok for a port call. It was to be over Christmas. The U.S. Army maintained a military hotel there, and we were able to get rooms. Lord, but it was lonesome. Everyone was homesick.

We met some Air Force pilots who were flying missions over Vietnam out of Bangkok. They were genuine heroes. Made us feel even worse, storming some unknown island like Tom Sawyer and Huck Finn while these guys were flying real combat missions every day and night. Their wives were visiting from Hawaii, and we took them all on a tour of the boat. They thought *we* were heroes to serve on a submarine.

Christmas day we were sitting in the bar drinking beer from cans and trying to build the world's biggest pyramid of empties. Really feeling sorry for ourselves. Suddenly, a soft voice asked to join us. Looking up, there was Bob Hope, in country to do one of his tours. He sat with us for a while, had a beer, told some stories, and genuinely lifted our spirits. Then he paid our bar tab. What a guy. Jane Fonda, eat your heart out!

Dog with Gravy and Other Delights

The Thai admiral threw a big formal dinner for us. Very fancy. It was on his flagship, an old, retired U.S. tin can.

The first course looked like white worms in a yellow-greenish sauce. It was fiery hot. Turned out to be fish guts curry.

The main course was a red meat shaped like a ham steak with the bone in and about half that size. Smothered in a thick gravy. Dog leg steak. Oh, god, what a meal.

On to Hong Kong

Hong Kong was pretty close by Pacific standards, and we were granted permission to go there for New Year's. En route we hit heavy weather and did not arrive until New Year's Day.

Victoria's Basin

We moored in Victoria's Basin, a tiny body of water protected by a sturdy seawall. The passage through the seawall gave us about two feet of clearance down each side. On the jetty was a Royal Navy band and a British officer with sword. Very impressive. We moored and he came aboard. After the preliminaries, he asked to see the executive officer. He told me I had a phone call from the States, it was not an emergency, and to call the overseas operator in Boston.

The Dragon Boat Bar

Stryker and I went ashore and got a room at the Hong Kong Hilton. I placed the call through the Hong Kong overseas operator. She said she'd call me back. We left word at the desk and retired to the Dragon Boat Bar to slake our thirst while I awaited the call. It was ten o'clock in the morning of New Year's Day in Hong Kong, eleven o'clock New Year's Eve in Boston.

Shortly, a messenger came to say my call was coming through. I could take it in the lobby. It was Pat at her folks' house in Massachusetts. They had had a bit of the bubbly.

As we started to talk, a Scottish bagpipe band began to parade the lobby. Kilts and all. Loud. Boisterous. Couldn't hear yourself think, much less carry on a conversation half the world around. Oh, well. It was still great to hear her voice.

Speaking of Phone Calls

In the late '60s, making an international telephone call was ponderous. I'll use the Submarine Sanctuary as an example.

First you dialed the Yokosuka operator. She put you through to the overseas operator in Tokyo. You gave her the number in the States, and she gave you an estimate of when there would be a free line, normally an hour or so. You hung up.

Later the phone would ring. The Yokosuka operator would tell you she had the Tokyo overseas operator on the line and transfer you. The

Tokyo overseas operator would transfer you to the overseas operator in Boston, who would transfer you to the local operator in North Hampton, Massachusetts, who would ring your wife. The whole process of transferring among operators could take five minutes. Now standby for the spooky part.

Have you ever picked up your phone to call somebody, only to have the same person already on the line calling you, answering you before the phone can ring? Most people have done so once or twice. You picked it up in the split-second after the phone connected but before it could ring to signal an incoming call. Unusual, but easily explained.

Overseas calls were quite expensive. Pat was pinching pennies at home. I was not throwing money around, either. Many nights I sat in the bar, homesick, wanting to call but not feeling we could afford it.

Twice, *I picked up the phone to call home, only to hear, "Hello? Is this you?" Pat was calling me from San Diego, and the connection had been made before the phone could ring.*

Spooky? You bet. Were we in each other's thoughts? You bet.

Back to Hong Kong

As I was saying . . .

Shoes

There were real bargains to be had in Hong Kong. One was shoes. Several shoemakers served the seagoing trade. You cut pictures from magazines to illustrate what you wanted. Then you picked out the leather you wanted. The shoemaker measured your feet and made a wooden mold. In two days the shoes were ready, and he kept the mold on file forever. Years later you could send him a picture and a description of the leather you wanted, and he would ship you the shoes.

You also could take along a pair of your wife's most comfortable shoes, and he would do the same thing. All for about $25 a pair. I bought some good dress boots for myself and alligator, snakeskin, suede, and other exotics for Pat. She still had one pair more than thirty years later.

Suits and Other Apparel

Tailors were also available. I had a new set of dress blues made and a black velvet opera cape lined with red silk for Pat.

The Vietnam war zone extended hundreds of miles offshore. Military personnel in the zone paid no income tax. We managed to sail through the zone as often as possible. Enlisted men got the full month tax free, officers only the days we were in the zone. It was our idea of tax reform.

Troops who reenlisted earned sizeable shipping-over bonuses at the time, often as much as $10,000. We encouraged those who were near the end of their enlistments to ship over early while we were in the war zone—tax free. This was a huge incentive. Anyone who might be eligible was marched up for a reenlistment physical before we left port. Those who chose to reenlist signed the paperwork while we were in the war zone and were paid cash on the barrelhead when we reached the next port, which happened to be Hong Kong in this case.

Suits, silk shirts, shoes, overcoats, handmade underwear, $10,000 bonus in pocket. Oh me, oh my. One sailor bought thirteen suits. Nehru suits, which were all the rage in some quarters. Standup collars, no lapels. Silk. Green. Purple. Suede shoes to match. Couple of pimp hats. Hell, it only cost him a couple grand. We always made the newly shipped dudes send a cashier's check for a large sum back to Momma.

New Year's Eve

Back to our arrival day. As you recall, we hit some heavy weather and did not make port until New Year's Day. Time for dinner. The entire wardroom proceeded to a famous restaurant. Decorations from the night before were still in place. Staff were visibly tired from the night before. Who the hell goes out for dinner on New Year's Day?

Skipper summoned the manager and told him this was New Year's Eve for USS *Volador,* an American by god *Man of War*. Scared the shit out of him. He mustered his troops, and off we went, complete with leftover party hats and noisemakers. New Year's Eve II for the staff. We had a ball. The tired staff got a big tip.

Jimmie's Kitchen

Hong Kong is a cosmopolitan town. Jimmie's Kitchen is a very sophisticated restaurant. We all went there for dinner the next night. El Capitano in the lead. Remember the departure from San Diego with the haunting strains of *"Please release me, let me go?"* He was not an imaginative diner, either.

We had an extremely efficient, somewhat obsequious Chinese waiter, who spoke impeccable English. Very formal. The captain ordered a Jack Daniels on the rocks. Bourbon in Hong Kong? The others followed suit, some with beer. I ordered a martini, very dry, Bombay gin. Bombay has a picture of Queen Victoria on the label. Very British. Hong Kong, right?

Waiter brought the drinks. When he got to me, he set down a martini glass full of gin, reached in his pocket, brought out an eye dropper of vermouth, and, with a flourish, asked, "How dry, sir?" Damn, I was in hog heaven.

Time to order. Old Himself orders a shrimp cocktail, rare steak, french fries, and a salad. The rest fell in line, some deciding for the baked potato. My turn.

"Vichyssoise to start, please."

"Very good, sir."

"Broiled trout for the first course."

"Very good, sir."

"I think lamb chops for the main course?"

"Of course, sir. Medium rare?"

"Fine."

"May I suggest a small salad after the lamb to cleanse the palate?"

"Please."

Time for dessert. Everybody orders deep-fried ice cream. They coat a ball of ice cream in pastry and really do deep fry it. Sorta like baked Alaska, Chinese style. Waiter never took my dessert order. Brought me a little tray with an apple, some grapes, and a hunk of cheddar cheese. Added a glass of cognac on the house.

Went back several times by myself or with Stryker. Same waiter. After the first time, I invited him to order for me. What a treat! Skipper never went back. Steak was tough.

Back to Japan: A Collision at Sea Can Ruin Your Whole Day

The holidays were over, and it was time to get back to Japan and get ready to earn our keep. As it was throughout the submarine fleet, the junior officers routinely made our landings for training. It had been a while since I had had a turn, and I asked the skipper if I could drive. He said OK.

Coming into Yokosuka, one proceeds up Sagami Wan (the entrance to Tokyo Bay) on the right hand side of the channel. Outgoing traffic, and it is heavy, passes to your left. Yokosuka is also on the left. When it comes time to turn, one looks for a break in the traffic and cuts quickly across the outward-bound stream of ships. Kinda like making a left turn at a busy intersection without a left-turn light.

At the appropriate time, I picked a spot ahead of a large outbound freighter and came hard left. As the turn developed it became apparent that the freighter was not a large one at distance, but a small one very much closer. And we were going to run into him!

"All back full. Right full rudder."

Bang! Hit him a glancing blow aft. Another ten feet and we'd have missed him. Shit! We stopped to make sure he was OK. He never even slowed down. We continued on into port.

We had suffered minimum damage. A fender-bender sort of wreck. Nevertheless, a collision is a collision. Not good for one's career. A Board of Inquiry was convened, and I was formally charged with "Negligently or willfully hazarding a naval vessel." I was warned I had the right to remain silent and to obtain legal counsel. I was informed of the maximum penalty, ten years in a naval prison, as I recall. The Board found me guilty and issued me a Letter of Caution that went into my service jacket, there to follow me forever.

We later found out we hit that little maru right in the officers' head, which was occupied at the time. Must have scared the crap out of that poor guy.

SpecOp Time

Time to earn our keep. Another SpecOp. Again, I can't say much, but the *Pueblo* guys were on our minds.

When *Scorpion* went down off the Azores, boats returning from SpecOps did not break radio silence until they were coming into port. That tragedy left wives and children waiting on the pier in Norfolk for a boat full of dead men. Afterwards, the policy changed, and we broke silence and checked in twenty-four hours before we were due to arrive. I made arrangements for the staff to call Pat when we checked in, and she would hop the next airplane out of San Diego. As it was, she arrived in Yokosuka before we did.

114

A Visit from Heaven

When we pulled in, Pat was waiting on the pier with the staff officers from COMSUBFLOT SEVEN. We had originally been scheduled to put in at Sasebo on the other coast of Japan, but had been diverted to Yokosuka.

The boat was wearing a half inch of green slimy growth. Stunk to high heavens. It had apparently grown during our extended submerged operations in warm water. Not to worry. We had thoroughly house-cleaned the interior, or so we thought.

Pat later said the warm air rising through the open hatches far out-stunk the slime. Said it would gag a maggot. Not us. We couldn't smell it. And no amount of scrubbing could remove it.

As an aside: I have no sense of smell to this day. I'm told many other diesel boat guys suffer the same malady. Our olfactory nerves just gave up, I guess.

We stayed the night in the guest quarters on base. Then took off the next day for our tour of Nippon. Benny the bartender had helped me plan the whole trip. My goal was not to see another round-eye. Get off the tourist path. Benny did a great job.

Three by Five Cards

The Special Services Office on the base existed to facilitate sailors' recreation. Many of the employees were Japanese. If you wanted to travel, they would book reservations, get tickets, and generally help with the planning. One particularly valuable service was their three by five cards. They would print basic phrases in English on one side, Japanese on the reverse. Useful stuff. For example, "What track is the train for Tokyo on?' Or, "Where is the bathroom?" Or, "Where is the taxi stand?"

When the staff thought we were going into Sasebo and knew Pat was coming to Yokosuka, they had a whole set of cards made up for her. I wonder if that kind of service is available in today's navy?

Anyway, we had our tickets and our translation cards and we were off.

Warm Bourbon

We stayed the first few nights in Yokosuka to get reacquainted. Benny had found us a small hotel never before seen by a Caucasian.

Mom-and-pop operation. We were met at the door by a smiling, bowing mama-san. Removed our shoes and donned slippers. Ushered to our room. It was delightful.

The room had traditional grass mat floors *(tatamis)*, a double futon, and sliding paper walls overlooking a garden. In one corner was a three-foot-deep hot tub. In another, a simple Japanese flower arrangement. It was authentic. No American tourist had ever been here before.

Benny had also found us some nearby restaurants. We went out for a lovely dinner. When we came back, we found our hostess had unpacked our luggage and hung up all our clothes. When she found our bottle of bourbon, she had thoughtfully placed it in an ice bucket of hot water. Hot sake, no? *Domo origato gazaimas.*

Mount Fuji

Next we went to Hakone at the base of Mount Fuji, the sacred Japanese mountain, actually a dormant volcano. Stayed in the exclusive old Fujiya hotel where MacArthur had established his headquarters after World War II.

The grounds included a beautiful pond full of huge goldfish. It snowed while we were there, an unexpected bonus.

I called and ordered a massage in our room for Pat. The desk, hearing a masculine voice, sent a woman. She was very embarrassed to minister to Pat. In Japan, men massage women and vice versa. Pat was just as glad they made the mistake.

There was a large private hot tub decorated with marble swans. We would take a bottle of hot sake with us, sit in the tub until well pruned, then submerge in a smaller tub fed with ice cold running spring water.

What a wonderful visit. All too short.

The Bullet

Next stop Tokyo. We boarded the high-speed train the Japanese call the bullet. Across the aisle was an elderly Japanese couple; she in a kimono, he in a western business suit. She reached in her voluminous net bag and produced a clothes hanger. He gravely removed jacket, tie, shirt, and pants and hung them neatly on the hanger. Then they sat, contentedly eating oranges, he in nothing but his skivvies. Saved wrinkling the suit.

Tokyo

In Tokyo, we stayed at a U.S. military billeting facility. It was full to the gills with guys on R & R from Vietnam. Made a number of new friends. One continuous party. Pat was a big hit. We really felt for those guys who were going right back to put their lives on the line. All too soon, the visit ended. Back to the real world.

Heading Home

Within a month, our tour up, we pointed the bow east and headed for the barn. San Diego, here we come.

The Zumwalt Navy

It was great to be home. Lots of things had changed. The kids had grown up. The antiwar demonstrators dominated the evening news. The hippies ruled southern California. And Admiral Zumwalt was the chief of Naval Operations.

Zumwalt issued policy messages, called Z-Grams, which completely changed the way things worked and rapidly were destroying the navy. He took the sailors out of the traditional bell-bottoms and Dixie-cup hats, and put them in pseudo chief's uniforms with silver buttons instead of brass. He authorized long hair and mustaches. He required every command to establish an ombudsman, to whom any sailor with a beef could complain, thus virtually destroying the chain of command. The staff had to establish a similar slot to hear bitches from the wives.

The chiefs and senior petty officers soon gave up, and the wives went bonkers. One evening, when we kept the crew aboard after working hours to prepare for an upcoming nuclear weapons inspection, we had wives demonstrating on the pier with signs reading, FREE THE VOLADOR PRISONERS. The troops thought it was a gas. The officers were losing control. And the Z-Grams continued to pour in.

Fire Hazard

One result of Zumwalt's haircut policy (*"anything goes"*) was a proliferation of Afros. We had one young kid on mess cook duty who had a head of hair like a bowling ball. He also had a wallet full of photos of white girls and delighted in telling the other mess cooks in detail how he had screwed each one. He was about to get himself killed, but I couldn't do much. His haircut was within regulations, and to tone him down would be racist. Luckily, our corpsman was black. He was responsible for cleanliness on the mess decks and inspected the cooks and mess cooks daily.

He counseled the kid to no avail. The corpsman was a soft-spoken South Carolina guy, and the kid was a mouthy Northern city boy. Not much in common other than skin pigment. Finally, exasperated, the chief declared the Afro hairdo a fire hazard and had the kid's head *shaved. Bald.* No racism here, by god. He probably saved the kid's life.

A New Skipper and the Drive of a Lifetime

We got a new skipper. Unfortunately, he did not last long.

Soon after he took command, we went up to Mare Island shipyard in San Francisco for some work to be done. One morning he did not show up on the boat, and we found him in his BOQ room lying in a pool of blood. A bleeding ulcer had let loose, and he was to be in the hospital for a while. We were due to go back to San Diego.

Over a martini in the submariners' bar the commodore asked if I was "qualified for command at sea?" I was. He asked if I would like to assume temporary command to drive the boat home. I was elated. Sorry for the skipper. But very few XOs got an opportunity to take a boat to sea. The division commander in San Diego was dying to look over my shoulder, but the commodore prevailed. Off we went. Heaven.

Hot Running Engines, Big Hole in the Boat

Mare Island is at the northern extreme of San Francisco Bay. As we sailed down the bay enjoying the scenery, word came to the bridge that two engines were running hot. We had left our torpedoes at Hunters' Point shipyard at the south end of the bay and had to stop to pick them up. So we limped in and tied up at the weapons pier.

We had been in dry-dock at Mare Island, and the engineer thought something might have been left in the sea chest (a kind of box alongside the keel where saltwater entered to cool the engines). The normal solution would be to request a diver to go down and look. But that would take a couple of days at least. Another, less orthodox solution, was to pressurize the engine room and go down from inside the boat. Which we did. When all the bolts were backed out and the circulating pipes removed, there in the sea chest intake was a coffee can full of nuts and bolts. Once it was removed, there was a perfect view of the harbor bottom through the open hole in our bottom. Only the air pressure in the engine room was keeping the water out.

We buttoned up and set sail. Sent a message to the squadron explaining what we had done. They were furious. We hadn't asked their permission. Screw them. I was in command, for however short a time.

Sailing under the Golden Gate Bridge was a real thrill.

On to Charleston

The navy brass had decided to consolidate boats of like types on the two coasts. As a result we were ordered to change our homeport to Charleston, South Carolina, "where the Ashley River joins the Cooper and forms the Atlantic Ocean." I had orders to the SUBLANT staff in Norfolk. I'd ride the boat around to Charleston and detach. Pat found a college student to drive the Volkswagen bus east and flew back with the kids to find a place to live. We got the boat ready to depart.

A new skipper was due. The old one was still under the weather. The new one was an ex-football player at the Academy. Only two years senior to me. I was looking forward to having a CO so close in rank.

Three days before we're due to leave. No skipper. Two days. No skipper. One day, still no skipper. He telephoned he was on the way. Was the boat ready to go? Of course. He said he'd arrive late that night and sleep on board.

Departure morning. The new CO is in his bunk, fast asleep. Left word he had gotten in very late and to let him sleep as long as possible. 0730. Due underway at 0800. Woke the Old Man. "Everything OK, XO?" "Yes, sir." "Very well. Get underway on time." And back to sleep. What a guy! Talk about building your XO's self-confidence.

We got underway on time, and the skipper arrived on the bridge, coffee cup in hand, as we departed San Diego harbor. "Thanks for the few extra minutes' sleep, XO. It was a long flight in last night." I knew I was gonna love this guy!

Rest Stops

Now, you should know that a cruise from San Diego to Charleston is long and arduous. Hard on ship and sailor alike. As a result, we were scheduled to spend a week in Acapulco, a few days in the Canal Zone, a couple of days in Kingston, Jamaica, and a final rest stop in Fort Lauderdale.

119

The Awning

We had off-loaded all our torpedoes and loaded a bunch of other stuff, so we would not be making our normal daily trim dive. We would make the entire run on the surface. In subtropical waters. Hot sun. Aha! Stryker strikes!

Before leaving Ballast Point (the San Diego submarine base), our erstwhile navigator was observed busily supervising some base repairmen in the area of the bridge. To all questions, the answer was "fuck off!" Not an unusual rejoinder from old Strykes, so I left him to his devices.

On the morning of sailing, there atop the bridge was a brand-new pipe structure topped by a gleaming white canvas awning. We were to cruise in style . . . in the shade. Since we weren't going to dive, it could stay up for the whole trip. And also because we would stay on the surface, Phil had installed a portable refrigerator under the awning to keep our beverages chilled. What a guy!

Arm Wrestling

As I said, the skipper was a big man. Biceps like small hams. Strong. I have biceps like willow sticks. Skinny. Weak.

Our first night ashore in Acapulco, we're sitting around having a few when the CO challenges all hands to arm wrestle. Couple of the more muscular guys give it a try and lose handily. Then he challenges me of the scrawny arms. The first time, it is almost a tie. He beats me with difficulty, then demands best two out of three. Tells the other guys I'm stronger than I look. This time I beat him, with difficulty. Then he wins for two out of three and demands three out of five. Lays $20 on the table and says he's betting on himself. The wardroom quickly covers, then raises until there's about $100 on the table. Only the CO has bet on himself. All the other money is riding on me. "Ready, Bruce?" Gleam in his eye. *BAAAM!*

Scoops up the money, cackling gleefully. "You guys are too gullible. Now you have paid for your lesson, and we will all recoup our losses in bars in the future. We will all bet on me, and we will get other suckers to bet on the XO." And we did.

The Panama Canal

First some interesting trivia.

The Pacific end is east of the Atlantic end.

The canal is gravity fed from Lake Gatune, high above sea level.

The water level at the Pacific end is about eight feet lower than the Atlantic.

If one were to bust the canal through at sea level, there would be a hell of a current trying to drain the Atlantic into the Pacific.

There is a narrow-gauge railroad parallel to the canal. It has open cars.

The railroad goes through jungle with monkeys in it. Great ride.

The canal is the only place in the world where the skipper is not legally responsible for his ship. The canal pilot is.

The canal transit was great. Everybody ought to do it once. I understand that even though the rest of Panama has gone to hell in a handbasket since we gave it back, the canal is still working fine. Just as Stryker's awning and refrig did.

The rest of the trip went fine. Nice port calls. We had bottled some Pacific water in small medicine bottles and labeled it "Genuine Pacific Ocean Water, Compliments of USS *Volador* (SS 490)." Sealed them with wax. Gave them to the crew to trade for drinks. It worked. They said they sometimes could purchase other local produce, too. We had turned the water into poontang for the troops. I stole the flag we had flown throughout the transit. Wanted one that had flown in both oceans.

But now I was anxious to get on with life. Charleston looked great. Pat and the kids were waiting. We hopped in the minibus in Charleston and headed for Norfolk and the new house.

Conference in the Driveway

The new house was great. Pat had done a bang-up job. I was ready to detach from *Volador* and report to COMSUBLANT as assistant intelligence officer. My new boss would be a full captain whom I knew only by reputation. I looked forward to meeting him.

There was a knock on the door, and there he was. Highly unusual. He introduced himself, and I invited him in. No, he said. He wanted to talk to me in the yard. Strange! As we stood in the driveway, he said since *Volador*'s CO was brand-new, and since I had more recent SpecOp experience than any XO in the Atlantic, I would be staying on board for a couple more months. Gonna take a little trip to sea. Leaving in three days.

I went back inside and told Pat I was going on a SpecOp in a couple of days. She would *never* ask where. All she asked was, "Want me to pack your long johns?" I allowed as how I wouldn't need them, and she knew where we were going. Navy wives are smart, and they read the newspapers.

Without violating an oath from which I have not yet been relieved, I will say a few things.

1. We were looking for Soviet submarines.

2. The water was, as always, shallow.

3. The dumb bastards in Washington put a destroyer in the same area with the same mission and *didn't tell him we were there!* We spent half our time evading our own guy!

4. All of our intelligence collection team were Russian linguists. *None of them spoke Spanish.* Luckily, we had a few crewmen who did.

5. After I got to SUBLANT, I did some research and found we were in violation of an old treaty by operating submerged in denied waters. *Nobody in Washington had thought to check with the State Department.*

But it was a fun trip, and I was due for two years on the beach. On to the SUBLANT staff!

COMSUBLANT

COMSUBLANT is a vice admiral and works directly for the Commander in Chief, U.S. Atlantic Fleet (CINCLANTFLEET). CINCLANTFLEET reports to CINCLANT, the Commander in Chief of all U.S. military forces in the Atlantic. In his CINCLANT role he commands Army and Air Forces as well as naval units. CINCLANT also wears a NATO hat as the Supreme Allied Commander in the Atlantic, SACLANT. COMSUBLANT supports him in that role, also.

The SUBLANT staff was housed in an old building on the main naval base in Norfolk. Unlike most other military staffs, where the Assistant Chief of Staff for Intelligence (N-2 on a naval staff) reports to the Chief of Staff, submarine doctrine delineated intelligence as a direct part of operations, so my boss reported to the Assistant Chief of Staff for Operations, N-3.

On many if not most staffs, the intell weenies, being coequal with the operators, tend to create their own fiefdoms and start writing intelligence analyses for their own consumption. Sometimes they even classify the product so highly the operators (read *users*) aren't allowed to see it. The Submarine Force had long ago decided that at the operational level, the *only function of intelligence is to support operating forces*. Therefore, they assigned the spooks to work directly for the operators. Clever.

Ours was a small shop. The boss was a captain. I, the assistant, was a lieutenant commander. We had one chief, one petty officer first class, and a seaman for a gofer. We worked closely with the CINCLANTFLEET intelligence staff. Our main purposes were to provide intelligence to submarines at sea, deliver a daily briefing to our admiral and staff, and manage the SpecOp program on behalf of the Chief of Naval Operations (CNO) in Washington, D.C.

It was a fascinating but exhausting job. Normal work hours were from 0600 to 1830 or 1900. We had to come in early to check overnight message traffic and build the admiral's briefing. On Saturdays, the boss and I traded off. One of us would come in at 0700, prepare the briefing, and attend the leisurely staff meeting in the admiral's mess. Very informal. Civilian clothes. The ancient (to me) captains, all in their early forties with nothing to do on Saturdays except play golf, would sit around and socialize over breakfast, normally until 1030 or 1100. On Sundays, one of us would come in sometime in the morning to check message traffic again, but their was no formal briefing.

Readiness, Politics, and Rank

Prior to deploying on a SpecOp, a submarine crew underwent an extensive training period called a workup. At the end of the workup, either the boss or myself rode the boat for a week and put them through their paces, after which we (hopefully) certified them ready to deploy in harm's way. Most of the skippers were commanders with an occasional captain thrown in. They were a talented and proud bunch. No problem for the boss to administer the graduation exam—he, too, was a captain and senior to all the skippers. But I was a lieutenant commander, junior to them all. To add to the potential for mischief, I have never by any standard been the soul of tact.

Most of the skippers had come up through Rickover's nuclear navy. They were first and foremost reactor operators. The best had been selected to be engineers on submarines, then instructors at nuclear power schools, then elsewhere in the nuclear world, with only short tours in operations, weapons, navigation, and so forth. Many felt that everything on board was subordinate to the power plant. We diesel sailors, on the other hand, believed the only purpose of the power plant, diesel-electric or nuclear, was to put our torpedoes in range of the target. Herein lay a basic philosophical difference.

As a result of their nuclear emphasis, some skippers were woefully inept at operational skills such as tactics, use of their electronic equipment, weapons employment, and periscope technique. For example, one skipper ran around at periscope depth, vulnerable to collision with any surface ship, for twenty minutes and never raised a periscope for a look around. Another never approached a target at less than thirty-five knots—so much for stealth.

Suffice it to say that I made enemies who were to haunt me later.

Secure Snorkeling

One boat was proceeding to station for a SpecOp. She was to remain undetected. The skipper, unbelievably, decided to practice snorkeling—in broad daylight off the coast of Canada.

A message from our Canadian friends flashed into SUBLANT Headquarters. One of their P-3 maritime patrol aircraft had spotted an unidentified submarine snorkeling happily along. Was he ours? Soviet? Not Canadian. Dumb shit!

Out flashed our message. "Secure snorkeling. Right full rudder. Come right ninety degrees. Make your depth 600 feet."

The guy just wasn't using his head.

Don't Eat Beets

Messages to submarines at sea were sent on a fleet broadcast at specified times. To copy the traffic, a boat had either to come to periscope depth or maintain a steady predetermined course deep while streaming a long wire antenna. Both actions severely restricted a boat's movements. To shorten the message stream, we reviewed all outgoing messages before they were transmitted. Some we kept for the boat's return. Essential ones were edited and made as short as possible. This was all to reduce the time the boat was required to listen in.

One message had to do with canned beets. The supply and medical corps had collaborated to produce a four-or five-page masterpiece. It identified said beets by manufacturer, lot number, date of canning, expiration date, wholesaler, navy stock number, ad nauseam. The medicos, not to be outdone, listed viruses, bacteria, symptoms, cures, and further predictions of doom.

What to do? We couldn't let our sailors eat tainted beets. But we couldn't burden them with this epistle, either. We condensed the message. *"Do not repeat not eat canned beets."*

When he returned, the skipper framed the four-pager and the condensed version side by side as a reminder on how to write. There's a lesson here for writers and English teachers.

The Navy Achievement Medal

When boats returned from a SpecOp they turned in a detailed patrol report along with various intelligence material they had collected. The raw intelligence material was sent to Washington for analysis. We reviewed the patrol report and wrote an endorsement before forwarding it to Washington. Then we recommended awards for the captain, selected crew, and the boat as a whole, based on the value of the mission.

The principal intelligence collected was electronic. Radio transmissions, radars and telemetry all required that intercept antennae be up and listening 95 percent of the time on station. Just tool along at periscope depth, don't run into anything, and keep those antennae listening was the goal.

One skipper, a senior captain, came back with about 3 percent antennae time. Every time he had heard something, *anything*, he had gone deep, cranked on the speed, and crossed the mountain to see what was on the other side. After all, he had all that *nuclear power!* Unfortunately, he collected almost no intelligence. His mission was a disaster.

Came time to write up his medal. I wrote him up for the Navy Achievement Medal, the lowest of all individual recognitions. Included elaborate praise—glowing prose. Only one problem, the NAM is restricted to lieutenant commanders and junior. This guy was a senior captain.

I routed the recommendation up the line. The boss's boss called me in. Told me the medal was for junior folks only. I said I knew that. This guy had acted like a junior officer right out of sub school. He smiled kindly and told me to write him up for a proper medal. *Then he told the son of a bitch what I had done, that I was right, and that the NAM was what he really deserved.* I had a new enemy for life and would pay the price later.

A Black Quartermaster

Because I was on twenty-four hour call, I normally didn't stand watches. However, in the summer months when lots of guys went on leave, I was called on to fill in. One night in the wee hours of the morning after umpteen cups of coffee, the young sailor who comprised the other half of the watch and I were discussing the ways of the world. He was extremely talented. Handsome. Well-spoken. And black. He said to me, "You know, Mr. Schick, I'm a damned good quartermaster. I do my job. I'll make chief some day. And I'm tired of being referred to as a good *black* quartermaster. Can't I just be a good quartermaster?" I've never forgotten that conversation. And he made chief.

The Dolphin Duckers

Norfolk is not far from Back Bay, in those days one of the premier duck hunting locations on the east coast. The problem was that the number of duck blinds on the bay were frozen. If one had an existing blind license he could renew it annually, but no new licenses were being issued. A chief on the staff, looking for a place to hunt quail, met an old retired Army warrant officer who lived on the bay and had three blinds. Bingo!

Five of us chipped in $100 apiece and formed a duck club. Had a white cypress boat hand-built, bought an outboard motor and trailer, and had enough left over to rebuild the duck blinds. Things were cheaper in those days.

We wrote up a set of bylaws and named ourselves the Dolphin Duckers. Elected a club president who would be known as the Head Mother Ducker. We had a ball and killed a lot of ducks.

Mr. Beasley, the property owner, had a six-car garage that was his hideaway. Kept whiskey in an old pair of hip boots. Mamma didn't allow no drinkin' in the house. After our hunts we would gather around his wood stove, drink whiskey, and listen to his tales. Fond memories.

Gasoline Rip-off

On the way to work one morning I passed an Esso station advertising gas at 40.9 cents a gallon. My god! I was so shocked I called home to report this obvious rip-off. Nobody would pay over 40 cents a gallon for gas! This guy was going to let greed run him out of business! Oh, well . . . at the Naval Academy I predicted stereo sound was a passing fad. Now we have $2 plus gasoline and five-speaker surround-sound systems.

End of Tour Treat

As part of a cooperative effort, the Royal Navy ran one SpecOp a year under American auspices. While the submarine remained under British control, we provided training, support, and guidance. We also provided a liaison officer for the trip. I begged to go, and my request was granted. I was to take a two-month ride in one of Her Majesty's nuclear boats.

HMS *Courageous* was designated to make the British SpecOp. Her skipper had been to Norfolk for extensive briefings and meetings with experienced U.S. skippers. I had come to know and like him. He seemed pleased when he learned I would be his liaison rider.

The Royal Navy

Time to fly to London for intelligence briefings from the Royal Navy. My instructions were clear. Under no circumstances was I to be identified as a U.S. Naval Officer. This was in-cog-nito, baby! Spook stuff! I was issued a passport and plane tickets in the name of George Washington. How original. Arrived at Heathrow. Baggage, of course, did not. Here I was in London with nothing but the clothes on my back. A guy showed up at the hotel wearing, honestly, *a trench coat and slouch hat.* Wanted to see my identification. Showed him the George Washington passport.

"No, your navy ID."

"But I'm traveling incognito!"

"Need to know who you really are."

"But who are you?"

"Can't tell you. Have to kill you if I did."

We finally got it worked out and he escorted me to Whitehall. I knew a bunch of the Brit spooks from my previous intelligence tour. They took me into a room full of filing cabinets and a reading table and then pointed out one cabinet that they said contained stuff they couldn't share with the U.S. They told me it was unlocked, but that I was not to go into it under any circumstances. And they would not be back for three hours. Wink, wink! Of course I dove right in. Sent a whole pad of notes back home in the diplomatic pouch. The Royal Navy and the U.S. Navy wanted to cooperate, but sometimes the higher-ups wouldn't let us.

Baggage finally arrived and I was off to Glasgow. As George Washington, of course.

HMS Courageous (S50). Photo courtesy of the HMS Courageous Society.

So Much for Disguises

I was met at the airport by a Royal Navy lorry driven by a chief petty officer in uniform. He stepped up, saluted smartly, and greeted me, "Good morning, Commander Washington." Oh, well. On to the base.

Checked into the BOQ. "Good morning, Commander Washington. Could I see your identification, please? No, not the passport, your navy

ID. Thank you, Commander Schick. Enjoy your stay with us." I was beginning to feel paranoid. Who was the real me?

They issued me a plastic card to hang around my neck. "Mr. Washington" it said. Gave me the run of the base. But I had to wear civvies. No uniform yet. Civvies were beginning to get a little ripe. Went down to the boat to look around. "Good morning, Commander Schick. Welcome aboard." Enough, already! Talked to my friend the skipper. Was loaned a Royal Navy uniform. I was now LCDR Schick, Royal Navy. Problem was I had a short haircut and a southern accent. Brits had hair like the Beatles and talked funny. But at least I was done with the civvies. And we soon put to sea.

Wine and Cigar Mess

I was invited to join the Wine & Cigar Mess. Unlike the U.S. Navy, the Royal Navy enjoys alcohol at sea. On submarines, by mutual consent, the officers use only wine and beer . . . no hard liquor. The troops are issued one beer a day. The officers pay for their spirits, their consumption being debited to their mess account.

How pleasant it was about a half hour before lunch when the skipper would call "Hey, Yank. Join me for a beer." Wine was served with meals. Senior enlisted men could save their weekly allowance for Saturday night. Junior enlisted had to drink theirs once a day. Never did I see the privileges abused.

How different from our ships, still bound by the bonds of Prohibition and the Bluenoses, where illicit alcohol is sneaked in dark corners without control or supervision. There may be a lesson here for bringing up teenagers, too.

Yellow Perils

Contrary to some restaurant reviewers, the Brits eat very well. Beef may have been a bit well done, but the lamb was great. So were the curries and fish. Soups were out of this world, particularly with a dash of peppered sherry added. Breakfasts were superb. But then there was the Yellow Peril, a.k.a. kippers. About as big as a trout. Bilious yellow color. Stank to high heaven. A Brit breakfast favorite. Tried one, only one. This Yank went back to bacon and eggs to the delight of my mess mates.

Sing for Your Supper

The commanding officer is never, by custom, president of the officers' mess. In *Courageous'* case, the XO was. Once a week was the President's Dinner, where he, rather than the captain sat at the head of table and presided. This meal offered a chance for a more informal setting.

At the first of these events, the president greeted me, "OK, Yank. Sing for your supper." Said I, "Sing what?" "You graduated from Annapolis. Sing your alma mater."

It had been fourteen years. I struggled through the first few lines and gave up amid much laughter from the mess. By the next week I had combed my memory and recovered the words, much to the delight of the same mess.

The Lecture

Saturday night was mess night for the crew. As mentioned earlier, the senior ratings were allowed to accumulate their week's beer ration. Some entertainment was provided and the crew afforded some relaxation and a break in the boredom of life at sea.

I was invited to lecture at a mess night, on any subject I chose, but "the lads would really like to hear about life as a Yank sailor, sir." At the appointed time I was met and escorted by the chief of the boat to the crew's mess. A mug of beer was shoved in my hand. "Beer's on us, Commander." I looked into a sea of faces that could have come from any U.S. boat. Hair a little longer, perhaps. Funny accents. But the same young faces. Talked for about three hours. Answered a zillion questions. Drank a lot of beer. What a privilege! Good sailors! Great shipmates.

The Patrol Report

The CO decided, given my intelligence experience, I would stand no watches but be on twenty-four-hour call as his personal advisor. And, to make up for my sloth, I would draft the patrol report. The report is drafted on a daily basis, not at the end of the patrol. Thus it is a work in progress. Problem was, I drafted it in *American, not English*, to the great glee of the other officers. Not to worry. Before long I learned to write *English,* mate!

At the end of the patrol, when requisite copies of the final product were produced, the skipper took a razor blade to the one which was destined for the U.S. He literally cut out sections which the British intell weenies had declared NOFORN (No Foreign Dissemination). This little ploy has always rankled submariners on both sides of the pond. The skipper was obviously embarrassed. After all, I had written the thing.

Then he produced another undefiled copy. Inside the front cover was a little envelope with a razor blade inside. This is yours, he said. Put in the U.S. diplomatic pouch and cut it up when you get home. What a gentleman.

Orders

About halfway through the cruise, the CO announced a special dinner. Coat and tie. Extra-fancy food. Several courses. At the beginning of the meal he said he had something to read to the mess. It was a message from the U.S. Navy Bureau of Personnel. He rose to his feet, donned his spectacles with great dignity, and commenced to read. It went something like this:

From: Bupers

To: LCDR B. J. Schick, USN

Subject: Orders

When detached on or about (date) proceed to the port in which she may be located and assume command of USS *Clamagore (SS343)*.

Then he said simply, "Congratulations, Skipper."

End of Cruise

In reading this section over, it seems I've said a lot about booze. Don't mean to make it a big issue, but that's where the memories reside. One more tale.

We were inbound to Glasgow. The boat sparkled. The men, too. Fresh haircuts. Best uniforms. High excitement. We rounded the sea buoy for the long leg into port. The wardroom table was rotated ninety degrees and the leaves were taken out. Then it was somehow lowered to make a very nice round coffee table. A secret cabinet was opened. Bottles of gin and brandy appeared. Mixers. Glasses. A small amount of ice. Celebration time. Homeward bound. Mission complete. Wives and girlfriends on the pier.

I ordered a gin and tonic. Steward opened a new bottle of gin, mixed the drink, recorked the bottle, and put it back in the secret cabinet. Think I'll have another. Same drill. New bottle, pour, recork, stow in the secret cabinet. "Have another, Yank." Same drill with the bottle.

Finally, I had to ask. What was going on? The queen was buying mine. One bottle at a time. Leftovers went to the mess. Thank you, Queen Elizabeth.

Command at Sea

Command at sea is the goal of every line officer, the culmination of years of work and study. Everything starting with Plebe Year at the Naval Academy would be coming together in this tour. Diesel boats were fast being replaced by nucs. Commands were scarce. In fact, *Clamagore* was one of only two diesel boats remaining in the Atlantic Fleet. She was homeported in New London, presently undergoing repairs in the Portsmouth Naval Shipyard. When repairs and her workup were completed, she was due to make a circumnavigation of South America on a cruise called UNITAS. Four months sailing the South Atlantic! I reported to the boat. Things were not so good.

USS Clamagore (SS343). *Official U.S. Navy photo.*

The Engines. As part of the repair work, the engines had been overhauled. New bearings had been installed improperly. When the engines were test-run, the bronze bearings had ground down, contaminating the engines with fine grit. Frantic efforts were underway to get rid of the contamination using ever finer filters.

Discipline. While routinely reviewing the boat's paperwork, I discovered a disturbing trend in the Unit Punishment Book. The number of sailors being punished at Captain's Mast was way too high.

Captain's Mast, literally Non-Judicial Punishment, is a mini-court-martial. The skipper is prosecutor, judge, and jury. While his actions are strictly limited by Navy Regulations, his power is large. For example, as a LCDR, I could fine a sailor a month's pay, confine him to the ship for a month, reduce him one rank, or put him in the brig for three days on bread and water.

There was a trend of sailors going absent-without-leave. When a sailor goes over the hill, he is declared a deserter at thirty days absence, removed from the ship's roster, and his case is turned over to federal authorities. In *Clamagore*'s case, sailors would go AWOL for twenty-nine days, return to the ship, go to Captain's Mast, and receive two weeks' restriction.

Twenty-nine days minus fourteen days equals fifteen days basket leave with pay. Some of the crew were on to a good deal.

Test Depth Dives. The boat had not been to test depth for the entire length of the skipper's tour. Usually a boat would go to test depth at least once a month to test for leaks and keep the crew used to the idea.

The Anchor. Same as test dives. Nobody on board remembered how to drop the anchor.

Morale. It stunk.

When taking command, a new skipper writes a letter to the squadron commander delineating discrepancies. Since I would have to fix same, listing all the problems seemed pointless, so I wrote everything was OK and signed on the dotted line. No need to embarrass my predecessor.

Worries. As you know from previous paragraphs, the predeployment workup is important. The date to arrive in Puerto Rico to begin the UNITAS trip was fixed. The engines were still fouled. The squadron commander was getting antsy. Making noises about substituting another boat. I begged. I pleaded. I spent every waking hour in the engine rooms.

Finally the lube oil cleared. The grit was gone. Off to New London.

Change of Command

Time for the big day. Everything was set up topside. The podium. The folding chairs with the starched white covers on the backs of the folding chairs. Friends and relatives invited. New frock for Pat, haircuts for the boys. And the skies opened up like a cow pissing on a flat rock! Emergency move to the base auditorium.

Outgoing skipper gives his speech. I read my orders. Turn to the skipper and say,

"I relieve you, sir.

He replies, "I stand relieved, sir."

Turning to the squadron commander,

"I have assumed command of *Clamagore*, sir."

"Very well. Congratulations, Captain."

What a feeling! My mother came on board for a tour. First time she'd been on a boat since *Irex*.

Workup

We went to sea. We went to test depth. Nothing leaked. We trained the anchor detail. We dropped anchor—repeatedly—until we got it right. The engines ran fine.

We loaded fuel and food. Installed a charcoal pit topside. Bought a skeet trap. Filled Safety Tank for showers. We were ready to go.

Henderson

Knock on my stateroom door. There stood a first class engineman, hat and service record in hand, in sparkling dress whites. His name was John Henderson, he said. Was being shanghaied to a nuc. Hated nucs. Needed a home—bad! Would work for passage. "Please look my record over, Cap'n."

His record was superb. His demeanor was above reproach. And we were stuck with a leading engineman who had just screwed up all our engines. This was too good to be true. Up to the squadron. Beg. Plead. OK—Henderson was ours.

Author's Note. Diesel boats generally had two types of engines: Fairbanks-Morse and General Motors. Those submarines built at Portsmouth had the former, those at Electric Boat in New London, the latter. All the boats I had been in prior to *Clamagore* had Fairbanks-Morse engines. They were basically locomotive engines. They had ten cylinders and twenty pistons connected to two crankshafts. They were very simple and reliable. The General Motors engines (Jimmies) were V-16s. They were very temperamental and threw oil everywhere. I knew little about them beyond what basics had been taught in Sub School. Like most submariners, I hated them. Henderson *loved* them.

Off to South America

Finally the day arrived. Last minute good-byes. Warm up the engines, take in the lines, and down the channel. We hadn't reached the railroad bridge when the first engine went south. Shit! Decided to continue and attempt repairs underway. Informed the squadron. They diverted us to Norfolk. Henderson and his crew worked night and day. The squadron informed us that the division commander (DIVCOM), my immediate boss, would meet us in Norfolk to conduct an investigation. Inauspicious start to a cruise.

Tugs? What Tugs?

By the time we got to Norfolk, the engine was fixed. Henderson reported that the diesel fuel we had loaded in New London was contaminated. As the diesel boats were being decommissioned over the past few years, their fuel had been offloaded into the base storage tanks. The boats were pumped dry, including the sludge that had accumulated over the years in the bottom of the fuel tanks. We had reported the problem earlier to the squadron. They could care less. They were all nucs—ran on nuclear power. Why worry about an old diesel boat? Bastards.

Sailing into Norfolk. Huge port. Told to moor alongside the submarine tender. No problem. Piece of cake. Easy approach. No current, not like New London. One of the junior officers swung in smartly, got the lines over, and landed light as a feather. Down came the tender duty officer, mad as hell. Where was our tug? What tug? Who needs a tug to make a landing like this? Any of my guys could do it blindfolded. *Regulations* in Norfolk *require* a tug. Another nuclear innovation. So sue me. The tender skipper came on board, hand outstretched (he was a diesel guy). "Haven't seen such sweet shiphandling in years. Congratulations! Welcome to Norfolk. What can the tender do for you?"

DIVCOM waiting. Grim. Why did the engine quit? Who to blame? Bad fuel? Oh, no. Must be somebody at fault. Even though he was a diesel guy, too, he had to appease his nuclear masters. No concept of loyalty down, only up. Brown-nosing bastard. Got gored running the bulls in Pamplona some years later. It's a sure bet the bull didn't get him in the balls . . . he didn't have any.

Pleasant surprise. The tender XO came on board. My old XO from *Razorback,* Joe Steckler. Good to see an old friend. Small world, the submarine force in those days.

The Propeller

Henderson again. He found out there was a submarine moored at Little Creek Amphibious Base getting ready to be scrapped. Anything on board salvageable was up for grabs. Wanted to take a working party over and see if he could scrounge anything useful. Why not? He borrowed a large truck and off he went.

Next day I was visiting my old XO on the tender. We were standing at the rail topside having a cup of coffee and watching the activity on the pier. Big self-propelled crane started down the pier. Joe said, "Wonder what that is? We don't have a crane scheduled for today."

A submarine propeller was dangling from a chain hooked to the crane. The crane was moving very slowly. Couple of sailors with ropes were steadying the propeller. My sailors! Henderson was driving! Oh, shit!

Down to the pier. Henderson waving cheerfully.

"Hi, Skipper."

"Whatcha' gonna do with the prop, Henderson?"

"Well, the tender had only enough scrap bronze to caste us six ship's plaques. This prop I found will make a bunch."

Four tons more! My old XO said if we'd give him the prop, he'd make us all the plaques we wanted and throw in the walnut backings. No mention that Henderson wasn't licensed to operate a navy crane.

Finally convinced the DIVCOM not to court-martial anybody and off we went to rendezvous at Puerto Rico.

139

The UNITAS Task Force

The UNITAS Task Force would be under the command of a rear admiral. It consisted of a big double-ended missile frigate, a smaller frigate, an old destroyer, *Clamagore*, and a P-3 antisubmarine aircraft detachment. To my surprise and delight, the smaller frigate was commanded by my Naval Academy roommate, whom I had not seen since graduation.

The UNITAS cruise was an event designed to provide training support to our South American allies and to show the flag. The cruise consisted of a four-month circumnavigation of South America with lots of time in port. We had excellent State Department support. They loaded us with trinkets to give away, hams, and cases of Johnny Walker Black Label Scotch, a favorite and very expensive in South America.

The admiral knew nothing about submarines except how to hunt them, but he knew he didn't know, and was a pleasure to work for. He stressed that the safety of *Clamagore* was paramount and let me run that part of the show. After a number of meetings among ourselves to iron out details, off we went, headed for the Panama Canal.

More Fuel Problems

We passed through the Canal uneventfully and stopped at the Naval Base at Colon to refuel and top off provisions. The base had no diesel, only jet fuel called JP-5, sort of souped-up kerosene. JP-5 will burn in a diesel engine. But it acts like a detergent, scouring any gunk with great efficiency. We had been trying to burn the contaminated fuel as best we could, but it was leaving a lot of residue in the fuel systems of the engines. We didn't need to introduce a potent cleanser to the problem. Across the canal was a huge commercial Texaco fuel farm containing thousands of gallons of pure, sweet diesel fuel. Priced to sell. But, no. We had to take on navy fuel, so we loaded up. Suffice it to say, the engine problem plagued us for the rest of the trip. The details are boring, so I'll not mention engines again. Ready for sea. Next stop Lima, Peru.

More about UNITAS

UNITAS was designed equally to train the South American navies and to show the flag. We spent lots of time in port. Every stop started with a ceremonial wreath-laying at the statue of the local/national hero. The host navy gave a big party for our officers and another for the troops.

We reciprocated by inviting the local dignitaries and their wives aboard for tours and dinners. Then our hosts would re-reciprocate, etc. Lots of parties. We gave away gallons of Scotch. They thought it odd we could not serve liquor on board. South Americans are *big* meat eaters. Tables would be loaded with a dozen or more types of meat and sausages. And bread. No vegetables. Not a balanced diet.

Operations consisted of coordinated air-sea antisubmarine operations. Our P-3 aircraft and surface ships worked with our host surface ships to try to destroy *Clamagore*. We spent almost all our time playing the target. The exception was entering and leaving port. Then we became the aggressor and attacked the departing or arriving fleet.

In order to be in position to attack a sortie, we would have to get underway early. Were we to be late, we would hold up the whole show. Embarrassing, to say the least.

I gave the word that any man arriving late for quarters would be fined $10 a minute. No questions asked. No excuses. This contrasted sharply with the previous skipper's policy of awarding a couple weeks basket leave. Naturally, the crew had to challenge the new policy. But I had to fine only one sailor. He was about fifteen minutes late. *Bang!* One hundred and fifty dollars. That sure puts a crimp in the next liberty. The troops quickly learned to look out for each other. I also told the chiefs they were responsible for getting their guys back on time.

Fire in the After Battery

Peru had state-operated whorehouses. Many of the troops were doing an all-nighter in one. Lots of booze consumed. Hard to get up and going (no pun intended). Couple of chiefs arrived in the early morning. Walked up and down the halls shouting, "Fire in the After Battery. All hands man your emergency stations."

I'm told half-naked sailors were popping out of doors like rats leaving a sinking ship. There's booze, there's broads, and there's fighting fire on board ship. Our guys were well-trained.

Everybody made it back on time.

The Driver's Pistola

Each skipper was assigned a car and driver by the host navy. The drivers were all chiefs in mufti. The XO and I were in the back seat going somewhere when the XO noted a large pistol on the front seat beside the driver. He asked the driver why the gun was on the seat. Driver replied it poked into his ribs when it was in its holster. OK.

Sombrero

Each of the ships was given a radio call sign for the trip. *Clamagore*'s was Sombrero. When visiting another ship, a skipper is "gonged" aboard. The ship's bell is struck (gonged) a number of times according to his rank, a bo'sun pipes him aboard, the officer of the deck salutes, and his ship's name is broadcast on the general announcing system, thus: *gong, gong. "Clamagore* arriving."

Our other captains took some liberties. The senior began to gong me: *gong, gong.* "Sombrero arriving." The Peruvians immediately picked up on it. Then at one of their big parties they gave me a straw sombrero, which I proudly wore with my dress whites to all formal occasions except wreath-layings.

El Bambino Capitano

I was thirty-six years old and baby-faced. Most of the South American navy wives I was to meet were much older. Many had better mustaches than I could grow. Most were plump—all that sausage and bread? But they were without exception a delightful, charming bunch. And they loved to tour submarines. Of course, we made a big fuss over them. The XO had immigrated from Spain and spoke fluent Spanish. He and I comprised our official tour guides. The ladies giggled and rolled their eyes a lot and joked with him in Spanish. Sombrero had another nickname: El Bambino Capitano. I was flattered.

On to Santiago, Chile . . . Almost

The Peruvians had been wonderful to us. Now it was on to Santiago, then around the Horn. But wait. As we were proceeding south we were told to hold up. The Chilean military, led by the navy, were staging a coup. We were to stand by for further instructions. I felt we were in no danger, but had a couple torpedoes made fully ready and tube-loaded. I had learned something from that skipper in the Iceland-U.K. gap. To a surface ship or aircraft, all submarines are black.

Finally, we were told to turn around and go back through the Canal to Uruguay. Seems our pilots for rounding the Cape were to have been Chilean naval officers, and in the eyes of Foggy Bottom, to embark them would be a *de facto* recognition of the new military regime. So north we headed.

Slow Speed and Ports of Call

The admiral called over on the radio. "How fast can you transit, Sombrero?" "On a twelve-thousand-mile leg, twelve knots." The destroyers normally traveled at about twenty knots. He asked if we'd be OK on our own. Surface ships usually travel in packs; submarines almost always alone. No problem.

OK, says the boss. See you in Montevideo. And off they went in a cloud of smoke. Shortly thereafter a message arrived telling us to pick two ports to visit on the way. He would fix it with the State Department.

Out came the guide books. I had promised choosing would be a democratic process, navy style. The officers could tell me where *they'd* like to stop, and I'd decide where we *would* stop.

Decision: Barbados and Recife, Brazil. Somebody got the bright idea of inviting the wives to Barbados. Technically, our movements were classified, but surely an exception could be made? We asked, and for once someone used some common sense. The visit was on. Back home in New London the planning began.

Barbados

A backwater of the British Empire that time had left behind. The wives, in their usual proficient mode, had rented an entire hotel. Old, sleepy, comfortable, off the beaten tourist path. Run by an elderly couple of Brit expatriates. We were the only guests, and our hosts treated us like family. We explored on bicycles, ate leisurely meals, drank some adult beverages, caught up on our sex lives, and generally relaxed. Although the navy frowned on it, we were just one big family . . . officers and enlisted. Even the bachelor sailors came by to participate.

The Bikini

I bought the spouse a little bitty bikini. Blue. Not much to it. We swam in the warm, clear water. I removed the top. Nobody could see us. We were in deep water. Oops! Dropped it. It sank. No problem. Stay where you are. Up to the hotel room to get a shirt for her. Two days later, the bra was hanging on the crew's bulletin board on the boat with a handwritten sign, "Lose something, Skipper?" The navy brass would not have approved, but who gave a damn? Our morale was higher than a kite.

Back to Work

After a delightful interlude, it was time to get back to work. Recife was uneventful. It's a huge merchant port—the closest point to Africa in the Western hemisphere. Lots of booze and whores for the troops, but not much else. Next: Rio de Janeiro.

Rio

In my opinion, Rio is the pearl of South America. Very cosmopolitan. The Brazilians viewed themselves as at the frontier of new development in the Americas, and I think they may have been right. We needed fuel. Badly. Clean, commercial diesel. No problem. Pulled up to a fueling pier. The charts were a hundred years old. Literally, there were handwritten notations by British sailing captains. We, being low on fuel, were drawing more water than usual, about nineteen feet. The chart showed nineteen feet alongside the pier, but the chart was *old!* No choice. We gingerly pulled alongside. Put the lines over to the pier. Started to haul on in. And the boat started to list. First a little bit. Then more . . . and more. The bottom was firmly stuck in the muck. We were aground! But as we pumped on fuel, it would displace water, we would get lighter, and we would float off the bottom. Back to our normal seventeen-foot draft. Bring it on! Commence fueling! It was far better fuel than we had been getting in New London.

The Sub Tactics Book

The skipper of the big, double-ended missile frigate was a senior captain, already selected for admiral. He was a great guy and a superb naval officer. But he was a surface officer, known to us as a "black shoe," or a "skimmer." He did things by the book. Everything was covered in the "book." I was whumping his ass. Had *sunk* his ship numerous times. He kept cajoling me, "Show me the submarine tactics book." I would tell him there was no such beast; we were taught to operate by the seat of our pants. Every sub skipper was different. This was a tradition going back to WWII and a central part of our success. He couldn't believe we didn't have a submarine bible to tell us what to do in any given situation. On one occasion, we passed close under his stern and took a photo through the periscope of the ship's name. We framed the photo and presented it to him at a formal dinner. I wore my choker whites and my sombrero.

Home for Christmas

The cruise was winding down. Christmas was approaching. We had been operating in warm tropical waters The bottom was covered with six inches of waving green grass. If we were to get back home in time for Christmas, we had to make some knots. We could catch the Gulf Stream off Florida to help, but we needed to hustle. So? Scrape the grass! We were parked behind a Brazilian aircraft carrier. The chief of the boat (COB) mustered an all-hands working party. Flooded down on one side to bring the other side up out of the water so we could scrape the grass off. Listed over about forty-five degrees. Tied ropes to the main deck, and everybody went over the side to scrape grass. All of a sudden down the pier came the emergency rescue unit from the carrier. They thought we were capsizing!

We scraped the grass, both sides, and picked up a knot or two. Time to head north!

The Backwaters

Back in New London, times were a little tough for a diesel submariner. The nuclear submarine force was predominate, and rightly so. Diesels were like dinosaurs. Relicts of the past. There were only two of us left, and, frankly, we were a pain in the ass to the higher-ups. Ironically, the remaining two diesel boats in the Atlantic Fleet were commanded by Tracy Kosoff and me, the last vestiges of *Irex*. We were well aware of our inferior status and went out of our way to irritate the nuclear guys, which included all of our superiors.

For example, the squadron commander had a regular meeting of his skippers early on Monday morning. Everyone was dolled up in dress blues with starched white shirts and ties. Spit-shined shoes. Waste of time. We were trying to get our boats ready to go to sea. Blaster and I would show up in the required dress blues, too, but wearing black drill shirts and big old fisherman sea-boots. Sometimes I would wear a British wool submarine turtleneck sweater I had acquired in

Courageous. Just to jerk their chains! Dumb, but fun. If you can picture a WWII fighter pilot, cockpit open, white silk scarf blowing in the wind . . . you can see us. The last of the dinosaurs. I can't speak for Tracy, but I was tweaking the tiger's tail and loving every minute of it. And I knew I would eventually pay the price.

Rising Waters

When alongside, the nucs always tied into electrical shore-power. They put huge cables over to a big connection box on the pier, hooked into Connecticut Edison Electric Power Company (CONED), and shut down the reactor. We rarely went on shore power unless we were going to be in port for an extended period. We just stayed on the batteries and charged them once a week or so.

It had been raining hard for weeks. The Thames was swollen and rising fast. We were attending the Monday morning skippers' meeting. The nucs, of course, were going to stay in port. School had been cancelled due to fast currents, as it were. Couldn't risk those valuable assets in a swiftly flooding river. The river was rising at a foot or so an hour. Current running about ten knots. Getting near the tops of the piers and *the electrical shore power distribution boxes.* Any diesel boat duty officer, much less skipper, would have recognized the imminent danger, cast off shore power, and gone back on ship's power. Not our prima donnas. They were all in a tizzy. What to do? Light off the precious reactors just to generate power for lights, heating, and air-conditioning? Reactors were made for bigger things.

Tracy told the skipper sitting next to him, "If the commodore will let me stay in port, you can run your shore power cables across the pier to me, and I'll light off an engine and power you up." Power a nuc with diesel-generated electricity? Horrors! It would be akin to infusing a knight of the Ku Klux Klan with pure Negro blood!

The meeting ended, we went to sea, and I guess Rickover's boys figured it out. Our nuclear commodore was, to say the least, not amused by his two bad boys.

UNODIR

I touched earlier on the differences in philosophy between the army and the navy. To reiterate briefly, army types are trained to look in the book for a reference authorizing whatever they want to do and usually telling them the way to do it. Navy guys, on the other hand, are taught they can do whatever it is they want to do unless the book *prohibits* it. Thus UNODIR.

UNODIR is electrical message shorthand for **Un**less **O**therwise **Dir**ected, as in, "UNODIR will depart current op area at completion of next exercise." UNODIR messages were used all the time. They were efficient. The superior officer need not reply if he agreed. It was generally understood they had to be submitted early enough to give the superior time to disagree and respond. But *early enough* is a phrase to warm a lawyer's heart, or as Slick Willie said, "It all depends on the meaning of 'is'."

We had been conducting weekly ops in Long Island sound. Boring stuff of some kind, probably enlisted sub school support. Due to come back in on Friday, but we finished everything early Thursday evening. If we hustled, the troops could sleep with Momma Thursday night.

Fired off a message something like this:

From: Clamagore

To: COMSUBRON 8

Subject Return to port

> 1. UNODIR returning to port immediately. Operations complete.
>
> 2. Request mooring instructions.

Not wanting to give the duty officer too much time to find a reason to say no, we sent the message as we were passing the sea buoy, inbound into the channel. By the time the staff radioman got the message to the duty officer, we were in sight of the headquarters building *What is the meaning of the word "is"?* The troops all got to sleep with Momma, the disgruntled duty officer ratted on me, and I had to listen to the commodore's lecture the next day. He didn't give a damn if my guys slept at sea when they could have been home in their own beds. Maybe that's why the nuclear boats' first-term reenlistment rate was below 10 percent and *Clamagore*'s was 72 percent.

UNODIR Again

Once again, we were on weekly ops in the sound and finished early. It was a little later than the last time, but we could be in by midnight Thursday, and the sailors would get at least a partial night home. Sent the UNODIR message in plenty of time this time. Waited for mooring instructions. Everything by the book. I knew the duty officer would be pissed because he had to come out in the cold, dark night away from his TV to see us safely alongside. And *Clamagore* was gaining somewhat of an unsavory reputation in the eyes of the staff, some of whom were on shore duty to rest their fat asses, not to service the boats.

Now Admiral Zumwalt was still king at the time. Haircut regulations were nonexistent. So, as we pulled alongside the pier in the dark, cold night, with the wind whipping and the poor duty officer freezing, *everybody on the bridge donned long-haired wigs!* Nasty, greasy, tangled fright wigs. Got to explain that the next day, too. Nucs have no sense of humor.

Bermuda

Tracy and I were doing a lot of training operations for sub school officers. The cruises involved two-week trips to Bermuda. A week down, diving and surfacing like porpoises. A weekend in Bermuda. And a week back. Easy ops and lots of fun. A chance to stock up on tax-free English woolens for the wives and duty-free booze.

On the way down one time, in a place called the Bermuda Deep (Bermuda Triangle by the press), we lay to, tied the boats together, lit off the charcoal grills (we were both from *Irex*, remember), and announced swim call for the troops.

Sailor on the bridge with an M-1 rifle to keep a shark watch. Officers, students, and sailors frolicking in unbelievably clear blue water. Charcoal heating up. Steaks on deck ready to be cooked.

A kid calls up to the bridge, "How far is the nearest land?" Jokester. OD replies, "Seven miles." Kid asks, "Which direction?" Reply, "Straight down." That was the truth. The water was seven miles deep. The kid came out of the water like he had a rubber band attached to him. Too deep for a farm boy from Kansas.

Motorbikes

Bermuda is a beautiful island, and a good way to see it is on a motorbike. There are a zillion of them for rent. Little underpowered things. But they can zip right along. And every sailor, of course, is a frustrated Indy 500 driver. Every skipper I had ever known recommended against letting the crew rent bikes. But Tracy was convincing—let the guys have some fun. OK. But I gave the crew a stern lecture. Any sailor in a bike accident would answer personally to me!

Later that afternoon Tracy and I are zooming down the road on our bikes between sampling the local bars. Hey, this is fun! *Bang!* Loose gravel. Over the handle bars into the gravel on my face. When I woke up, Tracy had my head in his lap scraping the gravel and blood out of my mouth, nose, and eyes. Off to the emergency room. Took a couple of hours to patch me up. Shunt in the hole in my leg. No skin on one cheek. One eye swollen shut. The troops loved it. Still have the scar on my leg.

Nuclear Torpedoes

We carried nuclear-tipped torpedoes. Nuclear weapons are serious business. Security requirements were elaborate and rigid. We had to meet both military and federal standards. Plans were in place to decommission *Clamagore* in a year or so, and personnel were in short supply. As a result, when sailors left the ship on normal reassignment, they were not being replaced. While this created some hardship, we were handling it. But suddenly we got to a point where we could no longer meet the requirements for the nuclear weapons security guard detail. We just didn't have enough bodies.

Talks with the squadron staff were not helpful. Their attitude was "suck it up." But the requirements were not open to debate. I asked that the weapons be removed. Denied. This was serious stuff. So I wrote a message:

> From: Clamagore
> To: CNO
> CINCLANTFLT
> COMSUBLANT
> COMSUBRON 8
> Subject: Nuclear Weapon Security
> References: (everything I could find)

1. Unable to meet security requirements of refs a thru x for nuclear weapons on board or guarantee their safety.

2. Request advise soonest.

B. J. Schick, Commanding

They came and took the fish off the next day and I got the worst ass-chewing I'd had in years for going out of channels. But the nuclear torpedoes were safely stowed on the tender.

Ensigns-in-Waiting

The nuclear fleet's appetite for personnel was insatiable. All the old preconditions for attending sub school had been scrapped. Now officers and enlisted men were arriving on the submarine base months before there was an opening for them in school. They normally were assigned busy work, and this was creating a minor morale problem among the young officers who were eager to get on with their submarine careers. To alleviate the problem, some of the boats, including ours, agreed to take a few of these ensigns aboard temporarily. They weren't much use, but at least they were living on a submarine. We would have two or three brand-new ensigns in the wardroom at any given time. They would stay for a few months until a school slot opened up, then they would be gone.

One day one of them read an article about ensigns on large surface ships. The senior, or "bull" ensign wore oversize collar devices engraved BULL. He was king of his little mountain of brown bars, all unofficial of course, but one of those little details that help morale. Our kid wanted to know if our ensigns could do a similar kind of thing, albeit there were only two or three of them. I said sure, why not? They promptly got a large set of gold bars engraved, and the senior guy pinned them on. One read BULL and the other read SHIT. When I asked why, they said that was part of the joke, being there were only two, not ten or twelve like on a big ship.

It turned into quite a little tradition. When the BULL got his orders to sub school, he would arrange a change of command ceremony at the club, invite the wardroom, buy the beer, and have a formal change of the guard, passing on the collar devices to his successor. Many of these kids, particularly if they were bachelors, visited the boat often while at school later on. We encouraged it. Sub school is tough, and they had a little hideaway on board where they could relax and find encouragement. To some, *Clamagore* had become their home-away-from-home.

I still have the engraved bars.

The Gathering Storm

Things were not going well. Nuclear submarines were unable to operate much of the time due to mechanical problems. Reenlistment rates were in the tank—somewhere around 10 percent. Officers were getting out in droves to accept higher paying jobs in the civilian nuclear sector. Navy training was worth a lot of money, and civilian reactors didn't go to sea for months on end. Cash incentives to convince junior officers to stay in had resulted in many skippers making less than their lieutenants.

I'm sure COMSUBLANT in Norfolk was under heavy pressure from his bosses. So the admiral and his senior staff were coming to New London for a big inspection, and the word was out they were going to kick some ass.

Our chief inspector was to be the force materiel officer (N-4), a very senior captain and former acquaintance of mine (see page 126).

The Inspection

A submarine, properly maintained, is cleaner than many homes. Nevertheless, inspections demand extra effort. We scrubbed. We polished. We painted. We perfected the paperwork. We were ready. The inspection party inspected. Very serious. Then it was lunch time. Steaks, of course. Starched linens. Attentive stewards. The head inspector sat at the table next to one of our temporary ensigns wearing engraved oversize collar bars engraved BULL and SHIT. The SHIT bar was, of course, on his side. Ever dropped a peanut butter sandwich? Which way did it land? Oh, sweet Jesus!

That Evening

When I got home, I mixed an extra-strong bourbon and water. I knew I was in deep water. After all, I had humiliated this man years before. And his boss, the admiral, was on a rampage. Then came the phone call. It was the squadron commander, another man whose tail I had been tweaking. I was to report to the flag suite at the BOQ at 0800 the next morning. The ass-chewing was a foregone conclusion. And there would probably be another letter of caution in my record.

The Bomb

I arrived at the flag suite as ordered. Droves of senior officers, all drinking coffee. Steward got me a cup. The senior guys were going out of their way to be nice to me. Something was wrong. They were too solicitous. The admiral arrived.

"It has come to my attention that you have been humiliating young officers by making them wear obscene, unauthorized rank devices."

"No, sir. They are wearing them by choice."

"But you condone it."

"Yes, sir."

"You are hereby relieved of command for demeaning junior officers under your care."

He turned on his heel and strode off. Every other officer in the room bowed his head and looked away. *No one would meet my eyes.* I was totally alone. I went home to Pat to break the news.

The Phone Call

The squadron commander called. If I wrote a letter stating that I could no longer stand the strain of submerged operations, the admiral would guarantee me a medical discharge from submarine service. No loss of face, no fuss, no muss, no pain, no scandal. But I was still in command and could still write messages.

The Clincher

This had been building for a long time. Deep down, I knew it. I just wouldn't admit it. I had done it my way, destined to lose my ass, and now I had. But I was still in command of a U.S. naval man-of-war. And I could write one final message:

> From: Clamagore
> To: CNO
> CINCLANTFLT
> Info: COMSUBLANT
> COMSUBRON 8
> Subject: Resignation

1. I find I can no longer support the policies of the Commander, Submarine Force, Atlantic.

2. Accordingly, I hereby resign command of USS Clamagore, and, in the best interests of the Navy, request you provide me a relief as soon as possible.

> B. J. Schick, Commanding

You can't fire me, you son-of-a-bitch. **I quit**!

The Ensign

The poor ensign wearing the bars was the son of an admiral and the grandson of an admiral. Good kid. He did his obligated time in the navy and resigned his commission. He blamed himself. An honorable man. The navy's loss.

The Relief

The troops were uneasy. Restless. Surly. Mumbling. The senior types on the staffs were concerned. Now *they* had a tiger by the tail. Who could they get to relieve me and not have the crew mutiny? Who else? Tracy Kosoff. And so it was.

Banishment

I was banned from the navy and sent to the Pentagon to labor in the pits at the Defense Intelligence Agency (DIA). All my submarine clearances were terminated. I found out later the submarine force had labeled me a security risk. I was approaching twenty years and put my retirement papers in. Life goes on. The new COMSUBLANT called one day and asked me to withdraw my papers. He wanted me to come down as his head spook. Promised he would see that I made captain. But it was too late. There was no more fire in this salt's belly.

He called once more to tell me that my old squadron commander, on the fast track for admiral, had been passed over. The admiral took the time to call him and ask him if he knew why. "Because you screwed Bruce Schick over, that's why." The admiral wanted me to know. Class act.

Postscript

So there you have it. *The Whale's Tales*. I wouldn't do one thing differently. As I sit here writing this, I think of the men I sailed with, the strength of the wives left behind, and how much the navy gave to all of us. Yes, we made sacrifices, but the returns far outweighed the investment. In the hustle and bustle of everyday life, I seldom think of the men riding our boats today, punching holes in the ocean. But they are there, every minute of every day. I know they are collecting memories as they go.

The Great White Bellowing Whale of *Irex* is dead now, buried at the Naval Academy.

Stryker died a couple years ago in Texas.

Blaster lost a long battle with cancer.

Pat died in the summer of 2002.

But somewhere out there on a submarine is a twenty-six-year old kid telling a nineteen-year-old kid, "Make your depth sixty-two feet. Up scope. Standby for a look-around. Mind your depth!"

Epilogue

USS *Razorback (SS 394)* was commissioned in 1944. She caught the tail end of WWII and continued to serve in the Cold War navy until she was decommissioned and sold to Turkey in 1970. The Turkish navy commissioned her as *TCG Murat Reis*, and she continued to serve until 2002, when she was retired and scheduled to be scrapped. Hearing of her impending demise, the city of North Little Rock, Arkansas, purchased her for use as the centerpiece of a planned maritime museum.

On May 5, 2004, she left Turkey under tow, having been divested of her diesel fuel, batteries and propellers. Her first port of call was to be New Orleans. Soon, thanks to e-mail, a couple of us who had served in her were in daily communication with the tug boat. As we tracked her progress across the Atlantic, we learned that she would make an unofficial stop in Key West before proceeding to New Orleans. We knew the New Orleans stop would be a big fancy deal with lots of hoopla. Not our style. But very few people knew about Key West. *Opportunity knocks.*

We were four. We had not seen each other since the late '60s—almost forty years earlier. We were, in order of seniority: Joe Steckler, the executive officer; myself, navigator and operations officer; Bob Denis, my relief as Ops/Nav; and John Cameron, who had served as gun boss and engineer. Two of us live in Virginia, one in California, and one in Florida. Logistical problems solved, we agreed to meet in Key West to welcome the old girl home. Bob and I would fly from D.C. and meet John flying in from California. Joe, who had some health problems at the time, would get his wife to drive him to our reunion.

Bob and I arrived at the airport. John's plane was due in about twenty minutes later. Would we recognize him? Forty years is a long time. We found him. Started to shake hands. Not good enough. Hugs. Bear hugs. Big, boisterous bear hugs. John shed a tear, I think. Then the banter started. Insults! Right where we had left off forty years ago. It was as if we had been apart for a weekend, not nearly half a century.

We got the rental car and went to find Joe. Then off to see *Razor-back*. She had arrived the night before. There she was! A little rusty, but still the same old girl. I think that's when Bob shed a tear. There were a couple dozen civilians milling about on the pier. We had figured whoever was in charge probably would not let us on board and were relying on Joe to do the negotiating, since he can sell freezers in Alaska. No problem. We introduced ourselves to the tow-master, and he asked if we would be willing to guide the eager tourists through the boat. Not only did we have access to the boat, we could explain her mysteries to our new civilian friends.

Below-decks was hotter than the hinges of hell. Couple of dinky fans to move the hot, humid air. Minimal lighting. But she smelled like home. Diesel fumes and human sweat. And memories of our youth. It all came flooding back . . . the valves and switches and machinery. The faces of the men with whom we had sailed. The camaraderie. The tourists were grateful, and we were more than a little puffed-up. We were professional killers once again, albeit a little bigger in the waist and thinner in the hair.

The watertight hatches were smaller and the ladders steeper than they had been forty years ago, but the people hadn't changed. Our guests were ordinary patriotic Americans, awed by this old black sewer-pipe. Grateful to the men who had gone down to the sea in her.

But enough was enough. We were hot and sweaty and dirty and thirsty. We terminated the tours, checked into the hotel, cleaned up, and got some dinner. Tomorrow would be another day.

Next morning we got organized. We bought a couple of cheap coolers, ice, a case of beer, and a case of bottled water. Off to the pier! Folks were already lined up for tours, but the guides (us) hadn't arrived. So we went to work. There were old navy veterans, young couples with children, cool cats with various body piercings and ponytails, and just plain folks. Universally, they asked, "Did you really live on this boat? It's so cramped. Were you afraid? Thank you for what you did."

We were having a ball. Joe's wife, Terry, arrived and we posed for a picture. Four aging warriors. Lumpy, but still proud. I think that's when Joe shed a tear.

The author, John Cameron, Bob Denis, Joe Steckler and grandson, Austin. Photo courtesy of Terry Steckler.

We sat on the pier. We told lies—sea stories. We guided more tours. We laughed. We had our pictures taken with the tourists. We had a few beers. In our hearts we were in our twenties again. Young and cocky and superbly trained. We were *submariners.*

Finally, it was time for her to leave for New Orleans. Single up the lines. Tug nestles alongside. Tug-master says he needs line-handlers. There we were. Cast off her mooring lines. It fell to me to release her last line and free her to the sea. *That's when I wept.*

Four aging sailors had been reunited with a part of our past, a battered yet proud old sea dog. She had been present in Tokyo Bay for the surrender in 1945 and had served off Vietnam. When nuclear technology made her obsolete in our navy, she served the Turks in a second life. Now she would become a museum for ordinary Americans to see and remember.

Were I a Marine, I'd say, *"Semper Fi."* But I'm not, so I'll just say, *"Diesel Boats Forever."* If you're ever in the area of North Little Rock, Arkansas, drop in and see her. You'll be glad you did.